# The Wiccan Temptress

# The Wiccan Temptress

*Marie Bruce*

ROBERT HALE · LONDON

*First published in Great Britain 2008*

ISBN 978-0-7090-8220-0

Robert Hale Limited
Clerkenwell House
Clerkenwell Green
London EC1R 0HT

www.halebooks.com



*A catalogue record for this book is available from the British Library*

2 4 6 8 10 9 7 5 3 1

Printed and bound in Great Britain by
Biddles Limited, King's Lynn

# Contents

# Prologue

You are about to experience the heady delights of magical sex, where witchcraft meets seduction, turning even the most ordinary woman into a super-sexy siren of enchantment! Gone are the days when women lay back and thought of England; a woman's role in sex is no longer passive and these days she is just as likely to take charge in the bedroom as she is in the kitchen or boardroom.

Sexiness is a state of mind, and all women have the potential to be sexy, regardless of their age, weight or shape. Being seductive is not synonymous with being a size eight (or, Goddess forbid, a size zero); nor does it require a boob job, nose job, face lift, collagen lips, hair extensions or any of the other surgical and cosmetic procedures Hollywood would like us to believe are the basic requirements for feminine allure. The way of the Wiccan temptress is much simpler, far less costly and invariably very effective.

I believe that any woman can learn to be a temptress. I also believe that every woman has a sultry secret siren hidden within her just waiting to be unleashed. The weapons in her arsenal include intellect, wit, a sense of humour, awareness of and a love of her own body, confidence, self-acceptance and an independent spirit. To all of these attractive qualities she may add the more mundane weapons of make-up and cosmetics, lingerie, smart clothing and luxury perfume, but there is far more to seduction than simply pulling on the right kind of push-up bra and the briefest pair of barely-there briefs! A true temptress can seduce a man at more than twenty paces with just a fleeting glance his way, for the look in her eyes ensnares him with a promise of what might be. She walks with a seductive sway, her smile holds an unspoken promise, and her eyes sparkle and gleam with a sexy secret.

Witches are naturally sexy and in the past they were often accused of ensnaring men with magic and enchantments, of seducing them with the help of charms and potions, and of taking revenge on those unfortunates who spurned their affections. Myth and legend are full of powerful enchantresses such as Circe, Morgan le Fey, Isolde, Vivienne, Rhiannon and Morrigan. Witchcraft itself has long been regarded as mystical and sexy, and to witches sex is a sacred act performed in perfect love and perfect trust – but that does not mean that we do not have fun with it! And when you weave together magic, sex and feminine allure you can become a very powerful witch indeed, one who can use her feminine skills to make the most of herself, to enhance her relationships and generally to make the whole world sit up and take notice.

Within the pages of this book you will find all you need to know about temptress magic and enchantments. You will find spells and rituals to ensnare, bewitch and seduce the man of your dreams. You will learn the secrets of the courtesans and temptresses of old, and you will feel the power of the Goddess tingling through you.

Here you will learn how to captivate as you caress, tempt as you tease, and charm with a kiss. In addition you will discover not only how to capture a man's heart and mind, but also how to hold on to him and keep him hungry for more, at the same time maintaining your independence, personal identity and mystical allure.

So pour yourself a cool glass of wine, slip into something more comfortable and prepare to be transformed into a sultry enchantress full of feminine power. It is time to free your inner temptress and experience the joy of magical sex – go on, leave him breathless!

Blessed be
Marie Bruce (Morgana)

CHAPTER 1

# Red-blooded Woman

Are you reclining provocatively? Then I'll begin ... Picture if you will a moonlit clearing in a dark forest of trees. A bonfire burns in the middle of the grove and all around it stand a group of dark-robed figures. One by one they cast a token into the flames and call out the wish of their heart. With each offering the flames dance higher, lighting up the expectation and anticipation in a dozen pairs of gleaming long-lashed eyes.

When each woman has made her offering to the flames they all throw off their cloaks and, joining hands, begin to dance around the fire. Slowly, seductively they move around the sacred grove in an ancient circle-dance, invoking love and passion into their lives as the fire consumes their magical tokens. The firelight glows on their naked bodies, now glistening with the first sheen of perspiration, and as the wood-smoke rises the shadows dance and leap around the tallest tree-tops, keeping perfect time with their human counterparts. Faster and more frantically the circle-dance continues until in a state of chanting, squealing ecstasy the coven of witches release the power that their dancing has raised and their love spell is complete.

Such is the stereotypical image of the sexy, beguiling witch, dancing skyclad around a midnight bonfire in order to summon a lover. It is a lasting image that has been portrayed in many guises via various different media and this sexy witch can be found in books, films, poetry and works of art. The *femme fatale* of witchcraft beckons to us from the pages of mythology and fairy tale; she smiles down on us from the walls of great art galleries; she whispers to us through song and commands our rapt attention from the silver screen. She captures the imagination of men and women alike, though usually for very different reasons. While men may dream of being seduced by her, women may find themselves wanting to *be* her. She is the ultimate temptress, and concealed behind all her fantasy folklore there is a very real truth which modern women are just rediscovering.

## The Sexy Side of Witchcraft

As a spiritual belief system which focuses strongly on nature, fertility and the equal polarity and duality of masculine and feminine energies, witchcraft cannot help but have a sexy side! All those ancient fire festivals and fertility rites which were designed to keep the earth growing green and to maintain an abundance of crops in the fields had to have a knock-on effect when it came to people's love lives and sexual relationships. Just try sitting on a hilltop all night waiting for the winter solstice sun to rise, or walking through a spring wood at dawn to bring in the May blossom, without finding a secluded bower where you and your chosen one can indulge in a spot of private fertility magic of your own.

Many of the tools and symbols of witchcraft are designed to represent the ultimate union of male and female energies. The sabbats themselves represent the turning of the Wheel of the Year, so honouring the fertility of the earth and the never-ending cycle of birth, life, death and rebirth. With so much emphasis on fertility and procreation it is hardly surprising that witches came to represent all that is seductive, beguiling and alluring about female sexuality.

In the past most rural areas had wise women to tend to the various needs of the community. These women were the witches of their day and they would act as nurse, midwife and confidante to the villagers. Often the wise woman would live apart from the community itself, preferring to keep a professional distance so that she might give good advice, for sometimes you have to be on the outside of a situation in order to have a clear view of what is going on. This distance from the village would often generate a degree of confidence from the villagers, leading people to confess their longings, yearnings and secrets to the wise woman, thus increasing her power and elevating her position within the community. It was to the wise woman that women would go for a charm to conceive a child, or a spell to turn a would-be lover's head. This magical knowledge of fertility and the cycles of nature reinforced the belief that witches knew more about sexuality and natural urges than most and that they had the power to ensnare the lover of their choice. Such beliefs helped to support the view that witches were powerful sorcerers of seduction, and so the mythology grew.

Of course these days witches tend to look just like everyone else and they are more apt to blend in than to stand out in a crowd. They may even be overlooked completely by their local community. Most modern witches have ordinary homes and conventional jobs, and lead pretty normal lives. They are just as likely to be seen doing the school-run as organizing a sabbat celebration!

But that does not make modern witches any less powerful than their historical predecessors. Today's witches use their magic to better their lives and overcome problems. It could even be said that modern witchcraft is self-help with a magical and spiritual twist. Many modern witches tap into the sexy side of witchcraft to enhance their relationships and bring about a desired result.

Unlike some of the more orthodox religions, in witchcraft sex has never been viewed as sinful or bad. Quite the contrary. Witches tend to view sex as a great gift and a very sacred act. We honour sex as a force of nature and so we can connect with the greater cycle of life and the heartbeat of Mother Earth simply by allowing nature to take its course and enjoying a sexual union with another individual. Having said that, witches on the whole do tend to take their sexual responsibilities very seriously, practising safe sex and ensuring that birth control has been discussed and is being taken care of. Most sex magic occurs between a committed couple, so reading this book is no excuse for behaving promiscuously or for taking risks with your sexual health and that of your partner. Be smart, be safe and respect your body enough to take good care of it.

Magical sex and seduction magic can be enjoyed by same-sex couples just as easily as heterosexual couples, but for the purposes of this book I will concentrate on heterosexual relationships. That does not mean that lesbian couples cannot benefit from its teachings, however, so just use your imagination and if necessary adapt the information to suit your own lifestyle and sexual preference.

By the same token, although I have written the book with a female reader in mind, men can benefit from reading it as it will give them an insight into female sexuality and they might even discover what makes a temptress tick – there are hints throughout the book which male readers can put into practice in their own love lives! And it would make a great gift for a girlfriend. Some men want to learn more about how the sexual psyche of the female works and *The Wiccan Temptress* can certainly help with such a quest. So girls, if you want to give your man a few hints, leave this book where he will find it!

It should be clear by now how and why witches gained a reputation for being a little bit saucy. Not only are we sexually responsible as well as sexually liberated, but we tend to be open-minded about sexuality, and we have a deeper understanding of the sacred aspects of the Earth's natural rhythms and fertility in general. But what about the notion that witches are involved in group sex and orgies? This rather titillating misconception came about during the witch-hunts, when simple fertility rites and celebrations of life, such as dancing around the May Pole, were considered to be virtually obscene – next time you are at a May Pole dance observe the wreath of flowers around the top of the pole and you will see why it caused such a Puritanical stir!

Another fertility rite involved riding a broomstick hobby-horse style across a barren field to encourage the growth of a bountiful crop. This gave rise to the belief that the early witches used their broom handles for sexual gratification and as the powerful energy of orgasm is sometimes used in fertility magic there could well be some truth to this. In their defence though I feel I should point out that this was centuries before sex toys made their presence felt, and if the ladies were having to trot up and down a muddy field for the good of the whole community then why should they not gain some pleasure for themselves along the way?

So all things considered it is unlikely that the kind of orgies that witches are sometimes associated with ever actually took place. Although this may disappoint some readers, wild sex orgies are not really what witchcraft and magical sex are all about.

## Skyclad

Contrary to popular belief nudity is optional within the Craft, not compulsory! As witches we refer to nudity within ritual as being *skyclad*, that is, clad only in the sky.

The human body is an awesome machine and for this reason alone it should be honoured and respected. Witches tend to place great spiritual value on the body and so going skyclad is all part of revering the human form in all its many shapes and sizes. Being skyclad is not about being perverted or vulgar, it is simply a way to connect more closely with the universe by performing magic in a natural state of nakedness. It should be said here that most skyclad rituals tend to be performed in the privacy of the witch's home or in a private, sheltered garden. We are not necessarily exhibitionists. When working magic out on the moors or in the woods witches generally wear dark cloaks, robes or their ordinary clothes, as nothing is less sacred than goose pimples, and the British weather can be unpredictable to say the least!

You should never feel pressured into going skyclad. It is a personal choice and you should wait until you feel ready before you reveal all in ritual, even if you work alone as a solitary practitioner or hedgewitch. As every woman knows there are days when the very last thing you want to do is fling off all your clothes and flaunt your goddess-given assets! We all have too fat days and too thin days as well as all the days in between. However, going skyclad in the privacy of your own home can help you to accept your body and to learn to love it unconditionally – something many women struggle with.

To be a successful temptress and a super-sexy siren you will need to be comfortable in your own skin. Being skyclad should leave you feeling blessed with the body of a goddess, not reaching for the latest slimming aid. Remember that goddesses come in all shapes and sizes too, just like us mere mortals, and think how boring womankind would be if we all looked the same. This book is not a guide to becoming a Stepford Witch!

And it can be difficult – but not impossible – to indulge in a steamy session of seduction without taking your clothes off! So the next time you are getting ready for bed, taking a shower or relaxing in the bath, tell yourself that you are the embodiment of feminine beauty and sexuality at its most alluring; you are skyclad and you are gorgeous.

## A Skyclad Blessing

In order to get the magical ball rolling and to increase your feelings of self-acceptance, try the following skyclad blessing. If at all possible stand before a full-length mirror as you perform it. Ideally you should be naked for this, but if you are feeling shy then peel off as much clothing as you dare, aiming to get down to your lingerie at least. As you work your way through the blessing say the words out loud and focus on that part of the body. Really look at yourself, even the bits you do not enjoy, and try to regard stretch marks and scars as badges of honour. Try to see yourself without judgement and find your inner temptress shining through. Allow your hands to wander freely over your body, re-acquainting yourself with your curves as you go. Take a deep breath and say the blessing slowly, pausing after each sentence to assess and accept your own unique beauty.

*Blessed be my hair that crowns my glory*
*Blessed be my eyes that reflect my yearnings*
*Blessed be my lips that pout a scarlet kiss*
*Blessed be my smile that holds a silent invitation*
*Blessed be my neck, awaiting a lover's kiss*
*Blessed be my skin, soft and smooth as satin*
*Blessed be my breasts which offer freely the milk of life*
*Blessed be my waist, lithe and supple*
*Blessed be my sex with its gift of orgasm*
*Blessed be my hips which gyrate in ecstasy*
*Blessed be my thighs which open the gates of love*
*Blessed be my feet which keep me true to my path through life*
*Blessed be my allure which makes me a natural temptress*
*Blessed be my body, for a goddess shines through!*

Repeat this ritual as often as you can and at least once a week until you begin to feel comfortable in your own skin. You may even find that it leaves you feeling a little frisky. This is perfectly natural, as once you begin to tune in to your inner temptress and goddess in such a way it is likely that this part of your personality will begin to demand some extra attention.

## The Wiccan Temptress

Just who is the Wiccan temptress? To put it simply, she is *you* – or at least, she is the magical seductress you have the potential to become. I view the Wiccan temptress as a confident woman, one who is in tune with her own sexuality and who is open minded to the idea of using witchcraft to improve her sex appeal and her sexual encounters.

The idea of woman as temptress is far from new. As an archetype she is an aspect of female sexuality and desire and her magic is as old as Eve. In essence, what I refer to as the Wiccan temptress is actually an amalgamation of various female archetypes from mythology, goddess iconography, folklore, fable and history. She is Eve shimmying her forbidden fruit in poor bewildered Adam's face; she is Morgan le Fey seducing King Arthur at the Beltain Fires; she is Guinevere beguiling her champion Lancelot with her charms; and she is Circe ensnaring her ex-lovers and turning them into pigs.

The sexy temptress also takes a hip-swaying walk through history, donning various guises as she does so, and in this sense she is Cleopatra cavorting with Caesar, and later with Mark Antony; she is Lady Emma Hamilton captivating Lord Horatio Nelson; and Wallis Simpson fascinating King Edward VIII into subsequent abdication from the throne. All these ladies are prime examples of the temptress at work. Whether these particular individuals seduced their men consciously or were swept away by love against their better judgement we may never know for sure, but one thing is certain: the end result was the same and each one of these ladies hooked her chosen man with all the skill of a champion angler! A woman's inner temptress, once aroused, is a powerful force to be reckoned with.

Men are quick to recognize the temptress in all her incarnations, from the shy teenager on the brink of sexual awakening to the thirty-something woman reaching her sexual peak, to the more mature lady with the knowing smile of experience. This should come as no surprise as most men have been secretly dreaming of the temptress since they were young boys of fifteen or sixteen in much the same way as women have been dreaming of 'Mr Right'. As adults, men are biologically programmed to pick up when a woman might be sexually receptive in the same way in which tom cats hang around the home of a queen when she is in season. This is the fertility law of nature coming into play, and it means that men are on the look-out for the seemingly unattainable beauty that might play hard to get but then makes the wait worth while! From the courtesans of a bygone era to the modern page three girl the temptress has fascinated men for centuries. While she may have changed with the times she has never disappeared completely and she is still at the core of every woman, regardless of age and maturity or youth and naivety. Below are three examples of modern temptresses in different stages of womanhood.

*Britney Spears*. She may be a troubled mother now but when Britney Spears first took the world by storm she was just fifteen years old and dancing energetically in a school uniform, the ultimate teenage temptress. She went on to become a global superstar with massive sex appeal.

*Nigella Lawson*. Nigella is quite possibly the sexiest thing an oven has ever seen. Not only does she make being a domestic goddess look easy, she manages to look fabulous at the same time as cooking up a banquet fit for a king. She is proud of her generous curves and rightly so. Men do not tune in to her show to watch her cooking a feast, they tune in to watch her eat it!

*Jane Fonda*. From her timeless role as the provocative Barbarella to her hugely successful work-out video Jane Fonda has had men drooling over her for decades and she continues to exude an air of sophisticated allure.

As you can see, being a temptress does not depend on youth alone, nor is it related to a particular dress size. You can be a successful temptress exactly as you are right now, for seduction begins in the mind and temptation can be wrought by exuding confidence, wit and charm.

## Media Glamour

I have an intense dislike of the images of idealized glamour with which the media bombard us. Such images of manufactured and air-brushed perfection do the female gender no favours at all and although we all know that we should not compare ourselves to them it can be difficult not to.

I am not saying that you should not have your professional portfolio or wedding photographs retouched, or that you cannot enjoy award shows and glossy magazines dedicated to celebrity and red carpet events. These can be valuable sources of inspiration when it comes to style tips and putting together your own ensemble for a special event. Try to remember though that underneath the designer dress the celebrity could well be wearing magic knickers that lift and tuck! The hair may look fabulous but how much of it is real and how much extensions? Be inspired by all means but try not to let unrealistic media glamour make you feel bad about yourself.

We all have insecurities, but a woman's greatest assets are her natural beauty and femininity. We will be looking at how to make the most of your beauty and enhance what the Goddess gave you a little later in the book. It is important though that you do not feel that you must be perfect in order to be sexy. Our imperfections can sometimes be very provocative and alluring indeed.

## Sexual Liberation

While an in-depth study of feminist politics is beyond the scope of this book it may be useful to understand the basic journey of liberation which female sexuality has taken. It is all too easy to take our liberty for granted and to imagine that a woman's life was always as free and within her own control as it is today, but of course nothing could be further from the truth.

There was a time in the past when a woman's body was far from being her own; it virtually belonged to her father and later to her husband. In wealthy families a young girl's virginity was considered to be an essential bartering tool in marriage negotiations, with the bride-to-be sometimes even being medically examined to prove that she was sexually pure and untouched. Only the poor were free to marry for love; in higher social circles marriage was a business contract, with the aim of benefiting both families.

Woe betide the high-born young lady who succumbed to a sexual tryst with her true love. She was likely to be disowned by her family, ostracized by her peers and maybe even confined to a convent. Young ladies were brought up to understand that their duty was to remain untouched until the marriage bed. Political betrothals may even have been formed when both the bride and groom were still infants.

Marriage brought about its own difficulties for rich and poor alike. Before the availability of adequate birth control women would go on having children year after year until their bodies could bear no more. Death in childbirth was common, as was infant mortality, and one can only imagine what labour and childbirth must have been like in an age where the medical techniques and equipment we take for granted today were completely unheard of.

Thank the Goddess that such times are long past! These days a woman is perfectly free to choose her own sexual partners, to marry for love or even to choose to remain single, hopefully without being regarded as pitiable. She is free to live with a man without the confines of marriage, or indeed to live with a woman if she is gay. Such freedom of choice should never be taken for granted and every woman's individual choice should be respected.

The real liberation of women came about in the 1960s with the availability of the contraceptive pill. Now not only were women able to enjoy sex without the fear of an unplanned pregnancy but they were also able to exercise a totally new power – the right not to have children at all.

Women were free to invent new roles for themselves as career women and business entrepreneurs. And of course such freedom changed their role in sexual relationships too, for now that they did not need to be tied down to one man in marriage and motherhood, they became free to explore their own sexuality more and even to enjoy a variety of partners. Until that point only men had been able to experience this. However, the sexual liberation of women also has something of a downside, which the young women of today are having to contend with.

## The Mark of Innocence

In today's media culture children grow up fast and virginity, once a highly prized treasure, is now regarded as being 'uncool'. Rather than being a sacred state of innocence, virginity is now something to be got rid of as soon as possible.

I have just recently turned thirty-three and I have noticed that young girls today seem to be growing up much faster than I and my peers did. When I was in secondary school there were fewer 'girls who had' than 'girls who hadn't', yet even I felt that my virginity was supposed to be a passing phase that I should have grown out of by the time I was fifteen – one year below the legal age of consent! I hated this form of peer pressure as I knew that I wanted to wait until I fell in love before having sex and I did not want to be made to feel as though I did not fit in because I was still a virgin.

Of course young adults will always be curious about the opposite gender, and about sexuality in general, for without such natural curiosity the human race would grind to a screeching halt. But many young people are now having sex without having first developed the level of maturity required to deal with all the emotional and physical repercussions. Teenage pregnancy is now so common that no one bats an eyelid at the group of young mothers hanging around street corners with their prams beside them. Such social problems will take years to solve but if we once more begin to regard virginity as a sacred state rather than a teenage embarrassment it may be possible to begin turning things around.

In the Craft virginity is regarded as a special and powerful time in a woman's life. Nor does giving that virginity to a lover mean that a woman has lost her purity, for purity exists in the heart and mind. While the term virgin is used today to denote someone who has never had sex, in witchcraft it carries a far older meaning and refers to a woman who is beholden to no man. I feel that this is a very empowering way to look at female virginity and we will be exploring this concept a little further in the next chapter.

## Sweet Seductresses

If you are still having some difficulty viewing yourself as a sexy seductress of Wiccan temptation then perhaps the following tales of red blooded women can inspire you.

## Cleopatra

Cleopatra, Queen of Egypt, is perhaps the most legendary seductress of all time, and not without cause. She knew how to use her sexuality and feminine allure to increase her worldly power and to get her own way. She successfully seduced Julius Caesar when he attempted to conquer Egypt; instead Cleopatra conquered him and their passionate love affair began! This affair effectively meant that Queen Cleopatra held the power of the Roman Empire within the palm of her hand, which is no mean feat.

Cleopatra considered herself to be a goddess incarnate. This is an ancient pagan concept, wherein women are regarded as holding a spark of goddess-divinity within them, a belief which still holds true in the Craft today. Cleopatra, being a queen as well as a goddess, acted the part to perfection and lived a life of pure, sensual goddess-like indulgence. Caesar, having come from the patriarchal society of Rome, must have been totally captivated by such a powerful woman, she who was completely in tune with her goddess centre.

After Julius Caesar was murdered, Cleopatra went on to fall in love with Mark Antony, using the very same seduction techniques which had so beguiled Caesar – reeling him in and then pulling away. She tempted both men not only with her quick wits, her sharp mind and her body, but also with her lust for power and her decadent lifestyle, allowing them to live the fantasy of making love to a goddess. Even at the very end Cleopatra refused to surrender to the power of Rome, and after Mark Antony's death, when the legions pounded her door, she took a snake from a basket and allowed it to bite her left breast sending the fatal venom straight to her heart.

## Mata Hari

As a successful exotic dancer Mata Hari travelled all over Europe performing for the elite of the time. When the First World War broke out the French decided to take advantage of her position and requested that she glean German war secrets during her interludes. And so Mata Hari would dance and cavort, seducing military secrets from the German officers. As she became more popular with the Germans, however, she began giving away French secrets too, becoming a double agent. She was arrested, made a full confession and was executed by a French firing squad in 1917.

Although she came to an unpleasant end her story shows that even governments and the military are fully aware of the power of feminine allure and sex appeal and, in this case, they were not above using a woman's wiles for their own ends.

## *Courtesans*

The eighteenth and nineteenth centuries were the heyday of the courtesans. They were rather like mistresses, but with one exception, a courtesan was kept by many lovers, not just one. Courtesans were high-born, well-bred women who had chosen a life of relative freedom over marriage. This could have been because they were impoverished members of high society and the decadent lifestyle appealed to them, or that they spurned the virtual prison which marriage was for the women of that time. Whatever their reasons, they were the celebrities of their day. They were glamorous ladies who were envied and admired.

The role of the courtesan was to entertain; she would give her time, her conversation and her body to the men of her choice, who could afford to keep her in the manner to which she was accustomed. In fact some courtesans were so rich that they were on a par with royalty, and royalty sometimes became their clients too. Their life was a whirl of parties, theatres and socializing. They moved in the very highest circles of society with complete independence.

Most courtesans used their assets to gain lavishly furnished homes, private carriages and their own boxes at the theatre, as well as money and jewels. Their homes were places of pure decadence; much like Cleopatra, a courtesan would seduce a man by tempting him into her private world of luxury and then billing him for the pleasure of the experience!

Far from being social pariahs like the street prostitutes of the lower classes, courtesans were highly regarded. They were the best-educated women of their time, and unlike married women could speak their minds on any subject and travel freely unaccompanied. They had many accomplishments and they were allowed to develop their knowledge, intellect and talents in a way in which married women were usually denied. Some even used their position to further their own personal ambitions; for example Veronica Franco became a published writer and popular poet.

When it comes to classy seductresses courtesans were the elite, the best of the best. They took the gifts nature had blessed them with and used them to carve themselves a place at the top of society, with the lifestyle to match. They were feminine sex appeal at its most powerful.

*One thing all these ladies had in common was confidence: confidence in their beauty, in their body and in their power to seduce a man – any man. They were all comfortable in their own skins and they used their sexual allure to increase their worldly power.*

*Modern temptresses can take a tip from these ladies by taking steps to increase their own personal confidence. You might like to pick out one of these famous seductresses of history to use as your personal role model, reading books about her and finding out as much about her as you can. Then put the more appealing aspects of her lifestyle into play in your own life. You will soon start to feel like a comely courtesan in your own right.*

*A tempting tip is to give yourself a truly gleaming smile like the beauty queens and smear a tiny amount of Vaseline across your teeth after brushing. Then dazzle everyone with your beautiful pearly whites!*

CHAPTER 2

# The Path of the Goddess

Witchcraft or Wicca is a goddess- and earth-centred religion, and is one of the main branches of paganism. This basically means that witches see divinity in the Earth – in the trees, weather, hills, meadows and oceans. In this sense divinity is all around us on a daily basis. Furthermore this also means that the religion of witchcraft is one which can be felt, seen, touched, smelt and tasted, as we enjoy the divine bounty of food and natural resources Mother Earth provides. Unlike the more orthodox religions, in which the divine is somehow above or beyond the humble believer, in Wicca we believe that a spark of divinity resides in every living thing and so we are in close contact with our deities every single day as we go about our business.

I believe that this strong focus on the divine feminine is largely the reason why so many modern women are being drawn to Wiccan ways and the magical path of witchcraft. Goddess awareness has even travelled as far as celebrity-land, with some very famous women speaking out about their interest in goddess spirituality, including Gwyneth Paltrow, Tori Amos, Pink and Cybill Shepherd. The re-emergence of the divine feminine is long overdue, as Dan Brown's best-selling novel *The Da Vinci Code* perfectly illustrates. As more and more women embrace the goddess path female empowerment becomes endemic, and in a society where women are taking on more and more responsibilities such empowerment can only be a good thing.

In the past women and men had very defined roles to play in life. Little girls were conditioned to accept the idea that they would eventually marry, have children and take care of the domestic aspects of home making, while young boys were taught that their role was to find a nice girl, settle down and go out to work in order to provide for the family. These days both genders have far more choice in life and the line between gender roles has become so blurred that one wonders if it still exists at all. You may find, for instance, that in addition to doing all the stereotypical female roles such as keeping house, buying groceries and taking care of the children, you are also taking on more typically masculine roles such as working full time, paying bills and organizing finances or taking the car to be repaired. This is especially likely to be the case if you are a single mother.

With such busy lives it can be difficult to find the time for a sex life or to go out and meet a new love interest. Yet taking time out to enjoy love and romance is essential to your well-being and your relationship, and it will help to keep you feeling feminine and womanly. Becoming a Wiccan temptress is as much a spiritual journey as a physical one, because sex is a sacred act. The way of the Wiccan temptress is a journey of self-discovery during which you will become reacquainted with your goddess-centre and your divine self. But first of all you need to identify your current relationship status to discover exactly where your temptress strengths lie.

## Single and Fabulous

The word single is no longer synonymous with the words sad and celibate. Single women are far more prevalent than they have ever been in the past, and they are more likely to be found at the very centre of a party than around the edge like wallflowers. Far from being regarded as being left on the shelf, single women today are viewed as taking their time in choosing a life partner, and they may even be enjoying playing the field.

Almost everyone will find themselves single at some stage in their lives and it is a phase to be enjoyed and embraced, not feared or resented. Having said that there are various degrees of being single, from the recently heart-broken to the 'between boyfriends and on the look-out' stage, to those individuals who prefer to live alone and are determined to remain unattached, yet enjoy going out on dates with men.

The hit TV show *Sex and the City* has virtually revolutionized the way in which society views single women – though it must be said that not all single women behave as promiscuously as the characters in the show! Yet the series does illustrate the new-found freedom of modern women in that marriage and motherhood are now optional.

I have been single for several years now, and some time ago I made the decision that I would not co-habit with anyone again as I love the freedom of living alone and the independence which the single life gives me. I exercise my right to remain child-free and, while I consider myself to be a single woman, that does not mean that I am without a man; indeed, not only do we enjoy some fabulous dates together, but I am the only woman I know who is regularly presented with bouquets of red roses. I am still single however, as is he; it is just that on occasion we choose to be single together, to go out and have fun and enjoy one another's company. In my mind I have the very best of both worlds. I am beholden to no man – as are many witches – so it was with some chagrin that I saw that following a recent interview with a journalist during which I had said that I was very happy with my life and enjoyed being single, I was misquoted as saying that I could not get a man! I received some very dubious fan mail as a result.

So just how does being a single woman affect your temptress style? The answer is quite a lot, for although you are free to flaunt your siren-self, you also need to be more careful in your flirtations than a married woman. Have you ever been to a party where you have been innocently chatting with a male guest, when his wife suddenly comes up and wraps herself around him in a grip worthy of a sumo wrestler? The message is clear: the affronted wife is silently screaming at you, 'This one's mine! Go and get your own!' What did you do wrong? Probably nothing, but in her eyes you either stood too close, chatted too long or laughed too provocatively in her husband's presence. And if she spends the remainder of the evening glaring at you from across the room then you probably did all three at once!

The simple fact is that your single status makes you a threat to other women, particularly those who might be feeling vulnerable about themselves or their relationships. If, for example, a woman is feeling a little sensitive about her age and you happen to be ten years her junior, or if she has recently had a baby, then your very presence is going to ruffle a few feathers. You might well be the most beautiful, talented and fascinating woman in the room, but you may not be liked for it!

Having said that, I do not believe that being popular with men necessarily means that you have to be unpopular with women. There is no reason why you cannot enjoy positive relations with members of both genders. But some women do seem to go out of their way to make enemies. I have no time at all for nasty, catty females. Just because you are female does mean that you have to behave like a bitch. Our nature should lead us to embrace the greater sisterhood of womankind. And at the end of the day it is far easier and lots more fun to be nice. So when you are in mixed company try to be sensitive to the feelings of other women and only flirt with single men! If a man really likes you then he will make sure he gets your number before you leave the event and the anticipation will only enhance the potential for seduction at a later date. By saving your full temptress style for a one-to-one date you will not risk giving away too much information too soon. The first rule of the Wiccan temptress is that you should always keep him wanting more! You can then sweep out of the party as the charming, mysterious woman who is admired by all, male and female alike, and who just happens to be single.

*By flirting only with single men, you will prove to other women that you are not a threat, and they could well be instrumental in introducing you to your dream man. Be kind to the sisterhood and the sisterhood will be kind to you! On dates, however, feel free to sauce things up a bit and be your siren-self, but remember to leave him wanting to know more about you.*

## Married and Marvellous

When the honeymoon is over the marriage begins, or so the saying goes. All marriages start off with a certain amount of anticipation and expectation on both sides. In the beginning the sex might be amazing as each partner savours the newly acquired 'right of ownership' and the knowledge that they have exclusive access to their partner's sexual favours. However the monotony of daily chores and the familiarity of living together can soon take its toll in the bedroom. Of course this is something that can happen to all couples who live together not just those who are married.

That said, the familiarity of married life can be turned entirely to your advantage as a temptress, for no one knows your man as well as you do. This gives you some power, especially when you surprise him by mixing something new into the familiar routine. When you are out together in public, married women can normally get away with being slightly more flirtatious than single girls. Nothing is more desirable than a woman who is desired by other men, and your husband may well take a strange masculine pride in the fact that his wife has captivated every man in the room but is going home with him. Needless to say, you should not take this too far – especially if you are married to the jealous type!

Other women are also slightly less antagonistic when married women flirt, as they know that at the end of the evening your husband will be taking you home. Of course, I am not advocating outrageous flirtation, and if someone looks hurt or resentful then you should stop immediately.

Another way in which you can rev your man's love-motor is to allude to a private joke, particularly one that refers to the bedroom, and then glance across at him with a twinkle in your eye. Discretion is the keyword however. You want your man eager to get you home so that he can repeat the private joke performance, whatever it may have been; you do not want to humiliate him and embarrass the crowd. The very best private jokes go completely unnoticed by anyone else, which is what makes them so sexy; it is private verbal foreplay between you and your man, in front of an audience.

Recapturing an aspect of your early married life can also help to keep things hot. If you used to walk through the woods together, or go dancing, or take long country drives stopping off for a picnic on the way, then start to do these things again in order to bring back memories and rekindle the old flame. And if you accidentally forget to put on lingerie beneath your long floaty dress, you can confess your mistake at an opportune moment! I know it is a cliché, but it is surprising the effect it can have on a man, especially when it is totally unexpected.

*A great marriage includes great sex and great sex involves variety and one or two pleasantly discreet surprises. As a married woman or someone who is living with a partner your temptress strength lies in your familiarity with your man. Use this familiarity to your advantage, but do dress it up with something new and different to surprise him, and of course to keep him wanting more.*

## Heartbroken and Desperate

The heartbreak of a romantic disappointment is a heavy burden to bear. While you may feel that all you want to do is lie beneath the duvet, crying into tissues and listening to the most heart-rending break-up songs, it is very important that you stay in touch with your family and friends, who will want to offer you support. Accept any invitations, even though you do not really feel like going out. You may think that all you want is to go unnoticed for the rest of your life and your greatest wish may be to become invisible, but never has it been more important to your self-esteem that you turn a room full of heads! And you don't need a man to be a temptress. It can often be very satisfying indeed to have every man's attention and yet to know that you are going home alone and that you heart is perfectly safe. And it can be a great boost to know that all eyes are following you out of the door. That has got to be good for your bruised ego!

Following a recent break-up dating will probably be the very last thing on your mind. You will need time to come to terms with things and to grieve for the loss of the relationship. Feeling desperately unhappy is all part of the process I am afraid, but it does not last forever and you *will* get through it.

Accepting your newly single status will be easier if you get out and about with friends. And it is vitally important that you get in touch with your inner temptress – not to find a new lover if you are not ready for one, but to increase your self-esteem and to keep feeling good about yourself. If Cupid has dealt you a harsh blow then you might need to go to some lengths to increase your confidence and your feeling of self-love and nurturing. Take up a dance or yoga class, go horse riding, have a make-over, go shopping for some new clothes which make you look and feel fabulous. A real temptress dresses for herself, not for a man. She takes steps to increase her femininity and to make herself feel lovely and womanly. She wears gorgeous perfumes and juicy lip glosses, but she does all of these things for *herself*. Male attention is just a by-product of her natural charm, allure and chic.

*Your road to recovery will be much easier if you tune in to your temptress-self, as this will increase your confidence and heal you from the inside out. Make every effort to feel good about yourself, and if you turn a few heads along the way then so much the better!*

## Find Your Goddess-centre

I have mentioned the goddess-centre a number of times, but what exactly is it? The goddess-centre is the core of your femininity. It is the sacred spirit of womanhood. Some of you will be familiar with the practice of opening and closing the chakras, which are the energy centres of the human body. In Eastern philosophy these seven chakras conduct the life force through the body. Each is related to a specific location on the body and also to a physical and spiritual aspect of life. Such energy centres cannot be seen with the naked eye, but they can be visualized psychically and they can be attuned with and worked with during meditation.

I am of the opinion that every woman has another energy centre and I like to refer to this as her goddess-centre. It is located in the womb area of the body, but as it is an energy centre it is not confined to the womb itself; women who have had hysterectomies still hold their goddess-centre within them.

Incidentally I am also of the opinion that men have a god-centre, where the core of their masculinity resides. This could explain why some men like to give a name to their penis; it could be that they are unconsciously tapping in to the strength of their god-centre!

For women the goddess-centre is the sacred hot-spot of womanhood. It is the energy centre where the first stirrings of desire are felt, where arousal grows and satisfaction explodes. When a woman is erotically charged it could be said that her goddess-centre is working overtime! But the goddess-centre is so much more than a sexual barometer. It is also the source of a woman's feminine power, for it conducts the spark of the divine feminine which all women have within them, and it sends that power through their bodies to strengthen and empower them on a daily basis.

It is essential therefore that you are in tune with your goddess-centre and that you feel connected to the divine feminine energy flowing through you. Some women feel this quite naturally – they are very tuned in to their body's natural rhythms, menstrual cycle and libido. However this does not mean that they are in a constant state of arousal; rather it means that they accept the quieter times of their cycle when their libido is naturally low, and they might use this phase to do something which makes them feel good about themselves, such as dancing, swimming or meditation. Some women may have a habit of sitting with the hands or even a cushion across their lower abdomen in an unconscious effort to protect their goddess-centre and feminine power source. If you are less in tune with your goddess-centre then you might feel cut off and isolated, at odds with your own body. Your natural cycles might become uncomfortable and you could view your period (or moon blood as witches tend to call it) as something of a chore you have to get through, rather than a phase of quiet time and rest before the cycle begins again. In being out of tune with your goddess-centre you are also cut off from your feminine power, your natural allure and possibly even your ability to achieve orgasm.

Fortunately you can connect with your goddess-centre in a number of simple ways, from meditation to masturbation. Keeping a close eye on your body rhythms, moods, menstrual cycle and libido can also help you to tune in to your divine feminine power source. In the meantime try the following exercise to commence your attunement.

### *Attuning with your Goddess-centre*

You will need twenty minutes when you will not be disturbed. You could perform this exercise while you are in the bath if that is the only private time you get. Ideally you should be skyclad, but you might prefer to wear a loose dressing gown.

Settle down comfortably on the floor and begin by closing your eyes and breathing deeply until you feel calm and relaxed. Now open your robe and place your hands on your lower abdomen, just below the navel. Keep your eyes closed and visualize your goddess-centre, the source of feminine energy which resides deep inside you. How you visualize it is a personal choice; you might view it as a red rose, or a pink love heart or a swirling orb of pink and red energy. However you see it, hold the picture in your mind and using the middle finger of your power hand, which is the hand you write with, trace small circles on your stomach, gently massaging your power source to life. Cup your other hand underneath, just above the bikini line, effectively supporting and nurturing the energy you are raising.

As you continue you should begin to feel a stirring deep within, similar to that of sexual arousal. Now visualize that the red rose is blooming, the love heart is beginning to beat or the orb is spinning steadily. Whatever your visualization is, add movement to it and then hold this image in your mind as you say the following incantation:

*Goddess-centre, deep within*
*I stir you now, let passions reign*
*Empowering strength of divinity*
*Fill me up with goddess-energy!*

When you feel the stirrings begin to travel around your body and you become charged with feminine energy, stop the exercise and enjoy the feminine power that you have raised. You might feel the urge to make love to your partner or to masturbate after this exercise. If so go right ahead and make the very most of the sacred goddess power within you!

You can enhance the atmosphere of this attunement exercise by lighting candles, burning incense and massaging sensual oil into your abdomen. None of these things is absolutely necessary, but they are nice additions if you have them to hand. Repeat the attunement exercise as often as you wish. You will soon begin to feel an intimate connection with your goddess-centre.

*It can be especially useful to perform this attunement just before you get ready for a night out, as it will put a spring in your step and a sparkle in your eyes, and it will give you a very seductive glow!*

## Discover Your Personal Goddess Path

The Goddess of witchcraft can be divided into three phases, each one being linked with a phase of the moon: the Maiden Goddess of the new and waxing moon; the Mother Goddess of the full moon; and the Crone Goddess of the waning and dark moon. I prefer to call the Crone Goddess the Dark Mother or Dark Enchantress, as I feel this reflects her temptress energies much better and it is also more flattering to older women!

Every woman passes through the three phases of the Goddess during her lifetime, beginning as a young maiden, moving through the mother phase in her early to mid-adult years, and then going on into the phase of the Dark Enchantress as she matures and becomes a wise elder. It is the feminine journey of life, and one which we all must take.

Each phase is then subdivided and given the various names and faces of mythological archetypes. So the Maiden might be known as Diana, Artemis or Persephone, the mother aspect might be called upon as Gaia, Demeter, Hera or Aphrodite, while the crone can be invoked as Hecate, Kali, Morrigan or Scota. In this way we are able to find a face of the Goddess which resonates with us and which we can relate to, bringing her that much closer to us in life and ritual. In essence though these are all a part of the one Great Goddess and the divine feminine energy of the universe.

In addition to moving through the three phases of female life as she matures, a woman usually relates more strongly to one aspect, and this is her chosen goddess path. Each path offers a wisdom of its own and each is equally valid. Having said that, each of the three paths presents a very different challenge and various lessons to be learned.

Discovering which goddess path you are on can help you to determine what kind of temptress lies within you, which goddesses of myth and legend rule your path, what your strengths and weaknesses might be and what all of this could mean with regard to your relationships and sexuality. So read on to determine which of the goddess paths you most identify with.

## *The Path of the Maiden*

The Maiden is the youthful Goddess of spring. When a young girl begins to menstruate she enters this phase and her goddess journey begins. In terms of age the maiden phase normally lasts until the mid-twenties or until a woman has a child. The Maiden is the virgin Goddess which can mean one of two things: either she has never had sex and so she is quite literally a virgin, or she is sexually active but considers herself to be beholden to no man, thus maintaining her independence and preserving her own identity. The latter is the more ancient meaning of the word and it is one that still holds true in the Craft today. As a witch you can consider yourself to be a virgin and still enjoy the pleasure of sex, as did some of the virgin goddesses; Diana for example had a romantic liaison with Endymion.

If you are on the maiden path your challenge will be to demonstrate and maintain your independence and accept total responsibility for yourself. Some maidens find this quite easy, while others might cling to the youthful aspects of a maiden's life well into their golden years. This can lead to the individual becoming dependent on others and having trouble taking responsibility for their actions, preferring to blame circumstances and people around them instead. Try not to fall into this trap if you are on the path of the Maiden.

Instead bring all the positive aspects of the Maiden to the forefront of your personality, such as independence, responsibility, optimism or a fun-loving nature. The path of the Maiden is not confined to young ladies alone though, and some older women might be on this path too. If so it is important that you take on the positive traits of the Maiden in order to enhance your seduction style, rather than manifesting the immature aspects of this phase. In fact the old phrase 'mutton dressed as lamb' could well have been inspired by older women exhibiting all the wrong aspects of the Maiden. Be youthful in your actions and your attitude, not in your attire!

Some lesbians may feel a strong affinity with the path of the Maiden, as obviously the idea of being beholden to no man would appeal to them and fit in well with their way of life. It could be for this reason that many lesbian witches choose to follow the Dianic tradition of witchcraft in which men are usually excluded and the rituals focus more heavily around the divine feminine.

However Diana is just one of the goddesses who rule the Maiden path, there are many others to choose from, including Artemis, Bloedewedd, Maid Marian, and Persephone. Try to read as much as you can about these and other Maiden goddesses of myth and legend in order to discover more about the nature of the Maiden archetype and learn from her legends as she dances with sylph-like grace, captivating men with her allure and her openness. She is honest and trusting, but she may give you a tendency to tantrums, which could be a turn off for your lovers, so watch that temper!

If you think that you might be on the path of the Maiden then your temptress style is likely to be classically coy; you are the innocent and provocative coquette. You might like to play the damsel in distress and dream of being rescued from your burning tower by a handsome knight in shining armour. Your seduction style lies in a big smile, wide eyes, a soft voice and a girly, flirty giggle. You might even want to try sucking obliviously on a lollypop – worked like a charm for Emma Bunton! Great role models for you are Marilyn Monroe, Audrey Hepburn, Kylie Minogue, Sandra Bullock, Anne Hathaway and the fictional heroines Scarlett O'Hara, Catherine Morland, Marianne Dashwood, Tess Durbeyfield, and the second Mrs de Winter.

## The Path of the Mother

The Mother is the Goddess of summer and the first fruitfulness of autumn. When a woman conceives her first child she enters the mother phase. In terms of age the mother phase lasts from the mid-twenties to the mid-forties, or until a woman reaches menopause. So even women who choose not to have children travel through the mother phase of life, although their maternal instincts may be directed towards pets, ailing parents or even a career in the care industry.

The Mother is the powerful matriarch of the family and even when her brood have grown up and had families of their own she may be reluctant to give up her role and even try to take control or interfere in how her children raise their own families. Goddess-wise the Mother is all abundance, creation and nurturing. Hers is the hand that strengthens the weak and gently guides those who might have lost their way. In life, this means a woman could well be drawn towards lost souls as she feels the need to help and guide them; whether this means fostering challenging children or helping the homeless, her philanthropy stems from her need to nurture.

When a woman is in the mother stage of life she is taking on greater responsibility. Coupled with the lesson of personal responsibility which the Maiden teaches, the Mother phase now embraces responsibility for all those she cares about, be they children, parents, a spouse or pets. It is during this powerful stage of life that a woman is likely to take full control of her destiny. Of course such responsibility can be quite daunting; it can be a very heavy burden for those women who enter the Mother phase before they are truly ready. Young mothers especially can feel quite overwhelmed by it all, as they have barely left their maiden days behind. But this is the challenge which the path of the Mother presents, whether you are ready for it or not.

Goddesses who rule this path include Gaia, Aphrodite, Demeter, Hera, Selene and Arianrhod. The Mother Goddess teaches us about the never-ending cycle of fertility, and the female menstrual cycle is her gift to womankind. Granted, there will be days when your moon time feels like anything but a gift, but the cramps do not make the monthly event any less sacred! Once again try to read as much as you can about the various myths of mother goddesses in order to gain a deeper understanding of this goddess path.

If you think that you might be on the path of the Mother and feel a strong affinity with this phase of the Goddess then your temptress style is likely to be very earthy. You will probably enjoy dates which get you out into nature and the fresh air, such as, beach walks watching the tide roll in, country cycle rides, picnics and pony trekking. You love to feel the wind in your hair and you might like nothing better than a genuine roll in the hay-loft! You might enjoy being pregnant, or plan to have a large family of your own one day.

Your seduction style lies in windswept hair, rosy cheeks, and a healthy glow. Your temptress tricks might include cooking a fantastic meal with which to lure a man into your 'castle perilous', skinny dipping in a natural lake, outdoor sex to spice things up a bit and wantonly flaunting your natural zest for life and love. Role models for you are Lauren Bacall, Katherine Hepburn, Madonna, Angelina Jolie, Nigella Lawson, Kate Winslet, and the fictional heroines Bathsheba Everdene, Cathy Earnshaw/Linton, Eleanor Dashwood, Annabel St George and Beatrice Lacey.

## *The Path of the Dark Enchantress*

The Dark Enchantress or Crone is the Goddess of winter. She is the Snow Queen and the Ice Maiden, the dark spirit of the sleeping earth when winter takes hold. When a woman ceases to menstruate she enters the phase of the Dark Enchantress. But far from being past her sell-by date, she is now free to enjoy a new lease of life. Many post-menopausal women claim to feel more sexually adventurous during this phase of their life and some even claim to have reached a whole new sexual peak.

But the path of the Dark Enchantress is not just for older women; some young women feel drawn to this Goddess path too, for this phase of the Goddess can be particularly exciting and powerful, as the enchantress is the mistress of magic. She keeps the greater mysteries safe and she is associated with the cycles of death and rebirth. As a wise woman she is a counsellor to her clan, the one who offers advice and wisdom to those who need it most. If you are on the path of the Dark Enchantress this will be clearly indicated by the number of people who tell you their troubles – even strangers.

Yet there is another side to the Dark Enchantress, a much sexier side, for she is also a powerful seductress with all the tools of magic and enchantment at her fingertips. This can be seen in some of the goddesses and characters who rule this path, for example Morgan le Fey, Morrigan, Hecate, Circe, Kali and Branwen – all very sexy women. Read up on these seductive icons to discover more about the path of the Dark Enchantress.

The challenge which this goddess path presents is to know yourself and be true to your own destiny and your own needs without causing harm to anyone else. Only when you know yourself at a deep level can you become truly powerful and the sole weaver of your destiny. In addition you must learn when to act and when to step back from a situation. This can be difficult when people are telling you their troubles, as it may lead you to think that you should take all their problems upon yourself, which will only lead to self-destruction. Instead you should try to help them find their own path, their own strength and therefore their own solution to their problems. This is perhaps the most responsible path of all for while the Maiden teaches you to be responsible for yourself, and the Mother teaches you to be responsible for a small family unit, the path of the Dark Enchantress or wise woman is entrusting you to teach the many people who will come to you for help and guidance, and it is your job to spread the wisdom in any way you can. So rather than taking care of the few, you will be teaching the masses. Such is the challenge of the Crone, and her path can sometimes feel like quite a solitary one.

The Dark Enchantress undulates through life, ensnaring men with her wisdom, power and independent spirit. While she might not need a man in her life on a permanent basis, she still fascinates them with her charm and she is not above using her sex appeal and allure to get what she wants from life. She mystifies just as much as she enchants, and she flits around like a butterfly, never allowing herself to be truly caught.

If you think that you might be on the path of the Dark Enchantress then your temptress style is likely to be the full vamp! You are the ultimate Wiccan seductress and your vixen tricks include ruby lips, long black lashes, intoxicating perfumes and come-to-bed eyes. You do not even need to say anything to your beau at all, for you can intrigue and beguile him with a single, smouldering look. You are the belle of the boudoir, reclining on a chaise longue in a negligée as you read erotic fiction, sip champagne and eat luxury chocolates – gifts from one of your many admirers. Men are clamouring for your attention and you love it!

Role models for you are Margaret Lockwood, Vivienne Leigh, Sophia Loren, Brigitte Bardot, Dita von Teese, Beyoncé, Dannii Minogue and the fictional vamps Lady Barbara Skelton, Vianne Rocher, Madame Olenska, Jane Eyre, Rebecca de Winter, Hester Prynne and Eustacia Vye.

## Personalize Your Path

As you can see, each of these goddess paths has a very different style of temptress. Once you have identified which you are on, play up to your unique temptress strengths to increase your seduction success. Of course some of you will exhibit aspects of each of the paths, which is also fine. Just notice what works for you and what does not. The trick is to incorporate these standard temptress tricks into your own unique personality, so do not be afraid to put your own spin on things in order to create a siren style that is totally and uniquely you.

For extra temptress kick try casting the following spell. It will help your unique temptress qualities to shine through. Sit before your mirror, gaze into the reflection of your own eyes and say:

> *Mighty Aphrodite I call on you, supreme goddess of love and beauty, to help me to become more sensual and enticing. I ask that you bestow your gifts of attraction and seduction upon me that I may tantalize and tease, excite and enflame my lover's lust for me. Let your vixen tricks travel freely through my flesh and let my natural temptress ways shine through, encouraging him to follow where I lead. In your name I do this deed. So let it be.*

This is the ideal spell to cast as you are putting on make-up and doing your hair. It can be enhanced by performing the goddess-centre ritual first, as worked in conjunction with one another they will make the very most of your feminine allure!

CHAPTER 3

# *Sex as a Magical Tool*

Sex is probably one of the most powerful forces in existence. This is true in daily life as well as in magic and witchcraft. From the heady excitement of falling madly in love to the more basic rush of lust to the loins, we can experience the power of sex on many different levels. All creatures on earth are governed to some extent by their sexual urges and their innate desire to connect with another of their species and possibly procreate.

As human beings we tend to consider ourselves to be above the more animalistic side of sex. We take our basic sexual urges to a higher level of sophistication – or so we like to think. We refer to the sex act as 'making love', and we engage in complex courtship rituals that romanticize sex and help to make sexuality in general more socially acceptable. At the end of the day, however, when we are very attracted to someone, our animal instincts kick in and we are happy to rut and tup with all the enthusiasm of our four-legged friends! And there is absolutely nothing wrong with this. Sex is one of the greatest joys in life, inducing a natural state of euphoria which then gives way to a satisfied feeling of deep contentment.

Have you ever noticed that the world seems to look much brighter through post-coital and love-drunk eyes? The sky appears to be a brighter shade of blue, the clouds seem fluffier and even the rain appears to be less grey. We may greet the world with a blissfully serene smile, or even a crazy grin, depending on how many orgasms were achieved! Sex is pleasure for pleasure's sake, and there is no truer act of love than that of sharing the intimate regions of your body with another individual.

It has been said that there is a very fine line between sexual and spiritual ecstasy, and that the power of orgasm is the closest humankind can get to divinity. In patriarchal religions, where sex and spirituality were kept entirely separate, this fine line was never to be crossed and engaging in 'sins of the flesh' was discouraged. At the same time procreation within marriage was encouraged, leading to something of a dilemma, as one cannot achieve the latter without first indulging in the former! In witchcraft, however, where sins of the flesh do not exist, we tend to erase this fine line altogether as we believe that sexual and spiritual ecstasy complement one another perfectly. We also hold the view that all acts of love and pleasure, including sex and masturbation, are gifts from the Goddess for us to enjoy. In enjoying and taking part in these gifts we also honour the Great Goddess and the Horned God, as well as honouring that spark of divinity which we hold within ourselves. From this point of view sex itself becomes a sacred act of worship.

## The Sacrificial Virgin

If you enjoy Gothic horror films then you are probably familiar with the image of a beautiful maiden tied to an altar and being helplessly subjected to the amorous attentions of her captor prior to her being sacrificed. Variations on this erotic theme can be found again and again in literature, art and film. Take for example the lusty vampire draining the life blood from the throat of his pretty young victim; or the demon perched upon the lifeless form of the swooning maiden as depicted in Henry Fuseli's painting *The Nightmare*; or even the screaming girl roped to the train tracks by the wicked villain in the heyday of the silent movie.

The sacrificial virgin has been portrayed in many guises and in many ways. She is the ultimate damsel in distress waiting for her faithful hero to rescue her and bring about a timely reprieve from death. This image of seemingly feminine frailty and vulnerability has captured the imagination for centuries. How many girls do not on occasion dream of being rescued by their dream knight? And what man does not picture himself battling against all the odds to win the hand of the most beautiful woman in the room? But who exactly is the unfortunate damsel offered up as a tasty morsel, and where did this lasting, if rather distorted image come from?

By and large the sacrificial virgin is a creature of myth but, like most myths and legends, there is a kernel of truth hidden within. It is thought by some that in ancient times, before patriarchal rule dominated, the reigning king would copulate with a pagan priestess in order to seal his union with the land. This divine union of king and priestess was supposed to ensure a prosperous kingdom and it was enacted for the good of the people and the country. It is likely that the priestess was picked out especially for the role, possibly even being of noble blood herself, and that it was deemed to be a great honour to enact this sacred rite.

Reference to this ritual can be found in certain mythologies, most notably the Arthurian sagas, in which King Arthur sleeps with the priestess Morgan le Fey at the Beltain fires, before realizing that she is actually his half-sister. In some cultures, most notably that of ancient Egypt, it was believed that a marriage between royal brother and sister would keep the bloodline strong and the kingdom thriving, although our modern mind recoils from the thought of such an incestuous union.

The coalition of royalty and pagan magic is thought to have taken place during the fertility sabbat of Beltain in the first year of the new king's reign, although some schools of thought say that it was an annual occurrence, to keep the land annually fertile and the kingdom thriving. Whatever its frequency, this type of ritual copulation is probably one of the oldest forms of sex magic ever performed. It has been both demonized and romanticized, giving rise to the popular and provocative image of the sacrificial virgin – though in all probability the only sacrifice that would have been made was that of physical virginity. It should be stated here that the idea of witches performing blood sacrifice is pure propaganda. Sacrificial victims, virgin or otherwise, have no place in the Craft.

## The Great Rite

The ritual sex act once thought to have taken place between king and priestess does have a place in modern witchcraft, and it is known as the Great Rite. It is the union of male and female energies within a sacred circle or environment. It can be performed symbolically or actually; in the symbolic rite the practitioner lowers the athame which represents the god and male energies, into the chalice which represents the goddess and female energies, in a sacred act of union. This is the way in which most solitary practitioners perform it in their rituals.

The actual Great Rite involves a priest and a priestess of the Craft making love within a sacred circle. Usually the couple are in a committed relationship anyway and so bringing magic into their sex life together is a natural step to take. It is a great way to raise power and to honour the divine within one another. In addition, and as a preliminary, the practitioners would invoke the god and goddess into their own bodies; this is known as drawing down the sun/god and drawing down the moon/goddess. In this way the practitioners become the earthly representatives of the gods for the duration of the rite, and it requires both participants to take an equal role in the invocations and the ritual. Needless to say, unless your partner is pagan or a practising witch you might find this kind of foreplay a bit tricky to explain! If you are in a fully pagan relationship however, then performing the Great Rite together can be a fantastic way to honour your relationship and your commitment to one another, in the sacred presence of your chosen deities. It can help to heal rifts and can increase the intensity of your passion for one another. It is especially useful to perform it if you are trying to start a family, as it will invoke the fertility blessings of the Goddess and the God. And if you are not in a relationship with another pagan, then try making a greenwood marriage (see below) instead.

## The Horned One

The Horned One is another name for the masculine deity of witchcraft. He is the witch's God and is in no way to be confused with the devil or Satan, which are Christian deities and have no place in the Craft. In witchcraft the Horned One is called by many names, among them Herne the Hunter, Pan, Cernunnos, and Dionysus. The horned god is loving and protective, charismatic and sensual. As a patron god of lovers he teaches a lesson of sexual patience and of the joy of giving pleasure as well as taking it.

As his title suggests the Horned One is always depicted sporting a magnificent pair of horns or antlers growing from his brow, and all horned animals are especially sacred to him. He is a god of virility, vegetation and fertility. He presides over the mating rituals of the entire animal kingdom, including us. Even today people might say that they are feeling horny when they are aroused sexually; this seemingly modern term has actually derived from paganism and the belief in the horned god of virility. While the essence of the horned god could be regarded as lusty and raunchy, this is by no means the same as masculine dominance, for both sexes have an equal part to play in any sexual relationship.

As a woman, working magically with the Horned One can help you to become more confident in your own sexuality and more self-assured with regard to your sexual prowess and your ability to attract. Although many women work regularly with the divine feminine, some tend to neglect the divine masculine, perhaps in the belief that he has nothing to teach us. In fact nothing could be further from the truth; the horned god of witchcraft can help you to become more assertive in the bedroom, bold enough to ask for what you want from a lover, and fearless in trying new things. Calling on him can also increase your chances of conception or help to bring a new love into your life if you are single. He can even help to spice up a flagging love life – if you are brave enough to follow where he leads!

## Blessing of the Horned God

To bring the energy of the Horned One into your life light a red candle and say the blessing below as you visualize the image to which you most relate, such as Pan or Herne.

*Horned One I call to you*
*Bring passion's heat my way*
*Let love's sweet euphoria*
*Lead my modesty astray!*
*No thought of what tomorrow brings*
*Living only for today*
*And as my lover's lust ignites*
*In honeyed rapture we will lie.*
*Rain your blessings on me*
*All your secrets, kiss and tell*
*Bring each day a blissful ecstasy*
*And lead me through Love's portal.*

Place the candle by the side of the bed and allow it to burn for a few minutes each night.

## Feeling Horny Spell

If you find yourself feeling frisky and want to give yourself the best chance of a night of fabulous sex, get the horned god on your side by repeating the following incantation as you envisage a night of passion with your lover.

*Feeling horny; don't ignore me*
*Fill me with delight.*
*Embrace this passion, Wiccan fashion;*
*Pan, keep us up all night!*

Let the candle burn as you prepare for a night of romance, then say the incantation once more just before blowing out the flame. Then brace yourself!

## A Greenwood Marriage

One of the most effective ways to seal a relationship and make the romantic bond stronger is to make a greenwood or sacred marriage. This is simply the act of making love out of doors in a wild and natural space. It is especially useful if your partner is not of a pagan persuasion and you wish to bring the essence of magic to your sex life without performing the Great Rite. This is also one of the strongest workings of fertility magic you can perform as the energies of the natural world around you will help to stir the seeds of your own fertility, encouraging them to bear fruit.

In the past country dwellers would often make a greenwood marriage prior to a conventional wedding in a church, and many a blushing bride has been secretly with child on her big day! In the countryside the old ways of paganism were slower to be swept aside, and so villagers honoured both the old and the new way of doing things. Usually a greenwood marriage would take place on one of the sacred sabbats of the year, Beltain in particular. This old pagan rite eventually passed down into country custom and it has even been referred to in literature by some of England's greatest classical authors, for example Thomas Hardy and D.H. Lawrence. (Who could resist Oliver Mellor's demanding request: 'Say you'll be mine in the woods!' Poor Lady Chatterley did not stand a chance!)

But what is it about a greenwood marriage that is so powerful, and why in a world of centrally heated housing and soft beds, do some people still feel drawn to make love in the woods? For one thing having sex outdoors takes us right back to our roots and our animal instincts are heightened by their natural environment. This can enhance the experience itself. And there is nothing more natural than to perform such a natural act in a natural landscape.

Indeed it can even seem as if the landscape itself is in collusion with you as a canopy of lush trees provides shelter, the velvet night enfolds you and your lover in darkness and the great heartbeat of the living earth rumbles through your body. What could be more romantic that a moonlit walk through the woods, hand in hand with you lover, followed by fabulous sex in a shady nook?

The greenwood marriage is a sacred act that binds two people together in a way that is often found wanting in conventional commitment ceremonies. It is the way of the Earth; the way of the Goddess, and it can make an ordinary relationship suddenly quite enchanting. Although a greenwood marriage is usually a spontaneous thing where you are caught up in the moment and nature takes over, a little careful planning would not go amiss, so do ensure that you find a very secluded bower for your tryst – there is nothing quite like a nosy dog walker to ruin the moment completely!

You might like to take a picnic along with you and enjoy a midnight feast after your exertions have worked up an appetite. Feed each other strawberries using large leaves as plates, sip a little oak-leaf or bramble-berry wine and really make the most of your elfin feast in the wood-nymph's grotto! Make sure that you leave the environment exactly as you found it, however, and clear away all your litter (including condoms).

Traditionally a greenwood marriage was sealed in the wood in that the couple would carve their initials in a tree trunk, or hammer a couple of nails into a tree and across one another to form an iron kiss. I do not advocate this kind of damage to trees but would suggest that instead you each take a leaf, flower or blossom and exchange them as love tokens. This is far kinder to the trees, which are after all the lungs of Mother Earth, and should be respected accordingly. Alternatively you could make your greenwood marriage beneath an oak tree and take an acorn away to plant in your garden at home. As the new tree grows it will help to strengthen your relationship and increase your love for one another.

If you are already married in a conventional sense, or have no plans for a wedding, you can still enjoy a greenwood marriage with your lover. This sacred rite is a fantastic way to deepen the bonds and enhance any committed relationship. It should not be undertaken lightly, however, as the two of you will be tied to one another by the deep magic of nature. Such a bond can be difficult to break if you later decide that you want to leave the relationship, so be very certain of your feelings for one another beforehand.

##  Sexy Sabbats and Festivals

There are certain times of year which are ripe for love and which can be most propitious to enjoy a little wildwood wantonness. For those of you who wish to indulge your 'wild woman of the woods' here are the most significant dates for your diary.

*The Eve of St Agnes, 20 January*. This is said to be the perfect night for having prophetic dreams of a new lover, particularly if you walk to bed backwards. It is also a good time for taking steps to enhance and improve a current relationship.

*St Valentine's Day, 14 February*. As everyone knows, St Valentine's Day is said to be the most romantic day of the year, so bring wildwood ways to your Valentine's date by taking a picnic outdoors or by walking hand in hand through the forest with your elfin lover or maybe just with your boyfriend.

*Ostara, 21 March approx*. Ostara is the sabbat which welcomes spring. The days are beginning to lengthen and we witness the fertility of the Earth as daffodils dance in the breeze and lambs gambol in the fields. This sabbat is sacred to the hare-goddess Eostre and eggs are her sacred symbol; it is not difficult to see how this sabbat was absorbed into Christianity and renamed Easter, making use of many of the original pagan symbols. Although the date of the Ostara sabbat varies very slightly year by year, depending on the date of the spring equinox, it usually falls on or around 21 March. Refer to my annual book *The Witch's Almanac* to discover the exact date on which it falls and then work your fertility magic, make a greenwood marriage with your lover and celebrate with lots of chocolate eggs.

*Beltain, 30 April.* May's Eve or the sabbat of Beltain was the traditional time of the greenwood marriage, when couples would go out a-maying, that is gathering the first may blossom branches from hawthorn trees, often stopping in a shady nook or quiet grove along the way. A great feast would end the day, with music and dancing round the May Pole and the Beltain fires, during which many couples would announce their betrothal and might even wander off for a second time! This is another fertility sabbat, during which we celebrate the beginning of summer. Lovers would take full advantage of the warmer weather, longer days and lusher grass. Beltain celebrations would continue into the next day which we still celebrate today as the bank holiday of May Day. As this is a fertility sabbat it is the ideal time to perform the Great Rite, to have a greenwood marriage, or for asking the Goddess to bless you with a child. Dancing around a May Pole or a Beltain bonfire are also said to improve your fertility and chances of conception.

*Litha, 21 June approx.* Litha is the sabbat of the summer solstice and as such it varies slightly from year to year, but it is usually around 21 June. This is the festival of high summer, when the days are at their longest and the sun at its strongest. It is a festival of the Horned One for at this time of year the woods are lush with vegetation offering lots of places to make a romantic interlude more magical. Other sexy traditions for this festival include making love within a stone circle or the phallus of the Cerne Abbas Giant. Both these practices are aspects of fertility magic and are said to improve the chances of conception. However, as people are generally more active and sociable during the summer months it may be wiser to wait until late evening if you are prepared to risk outdoor fertility sex at a sacred site in midsummer.

*Samhain, 31 October.* Although Samhain, or Halloween as it is known among non-witches, is not a fertility festival but one of harvest, it is considered to be the most powerful time for witches and many powerful love spells can be cast upon this bewitching night. I am sure many of you will have peeled an apple and then thrown the peel over your shoulder to see what initial it makes on landing; this is thought to be the initial of the first name of your future true love. Another spell says that you should eat a shiny red apple in front of a mirror while brushing your hair to see a vision of your future husband in the looking glass before you. How blissfully romantic! It is also thought that fear can enhance sexual arousal, so if all you do on Halloween night is go to see a scary film, be sure to wear your sexiest lingerie and then cling helplessly to your date throughout. If he is too busy hiding behind your handbag to notice, however, then perhaps he is not the one after all. Alternatively go for a spooky walk in the dark, dark woods; go camping and tell ghost stories and urban legends with a sexy twist around the campfire; or just stay at home, adding a seasonal and saucy twist to your evening by dressing up as Dracula and his bride.

*Yule, 21 December approx.* Yule is the sabbat of the winter solstice and the date varies from year to year, usually falling around 21 December. The days are dark and chilly and the winter solstice is the longest night of the whole year, with more than twelve hours of darkness. This is the ideal time for cocooning with your partner in a cosy love nest of your own creation, so cuddle up before the fire, drink mulled wine and feed one another treats. The tradition of bringing greenery into the house for Yuletide was to remind people of the endless bounty of nature and the promise that spring was just a few months away. But more than that, specific plants represented the fertility of the Earth Goddess and the Horned God. Holly, for example, represents the God while ivy represents the Goddess. Twining these two plants together is said to encourage fertility, fidelity and the longevity of a relationship. Mistletoe is of course more commonly known as the kissing bough and most women have had a kiss or two stolen from them beneath it at some time or another! The round-edged, curvaceous leaves represent the Goddess and the white berries the seed of the Horned God. Each berry is the gift of a kiss and for every kiss taken a single berry must be removed. As soon as all the berries are gone then the kissing should stop.

*New Year's Eve, 31 December*. This is another festival of kissing. The death of the old year and the birth of the new one is the perfect excuse for a snog-fest! It might give you the opportunity to kiss someone you have fancied for months, or you could give a handsome stranger a peck on the cheek before drifting off into the night like the exotic and mysterious creature you are. Alternatively, you may simply choose to indulge in a night of fun and frolics with your long-term lover. Whatever you decide to do, make the most of your luscious lips. Although the actual passing of one year into the next is the briefest moment in time, you will notice that the kissing tends to go on for much longer!

*A Bride's moon*. When the moon is new to waxing it is sometimes referred to as a Bride's moon. Bride is the Celtic virgin goddess of the spring, and she is the patron goddess of writers and poets. She is also associated with fire and all forms of literature, particularly epic poetry. The night of a Bride's moon is the ideal time for a first date, a marriage proposal, a fresh start between long-term lovers, or an exciting new phase within an existing relationship. Now is the time to make exciting new plans with your lover or even to read poetry together. Or be really romantic and write a poem for your true love. Romantic meals enjoyed at this time of the lunar cycle can be enhanced by burning silver candles to honour Bride and to echo the crescent light of the Bride's moon.

*A lover's moon*. As the Bride's moon swells to full it is romantically referred to as the lover's moon, possibly because its enchanting light encourages moonlit walks, serenades, long, lingering goodnight kisses and wishes on stars while gazing heavenwards. As the full moon has a magnetic pull on the tide this can often be the most romantic time to visit the coast, where you can sit on the seashore and watch the bright orb of a lover's moon rise up over the ocean surf. Other ways in which you can enjoy the romance of this lunar phase include camping out in a meadow, or reclining together in a garden hammock. Magically speaking the full moon is the most powerful lunar phase of all, so any seduction magic performed at this time will be greatly enhanced.

As you can see, there are plenty of opportunities throughout the year for you to take advantage of seasonal and lunar energies in order to strengthen and enhance your temptress ways. Make a note in your diary of the next sacred time and start to plan your great seduction!

##  Sex as a Power Source

Sex can provide a tremendous power boost to your rituals. Indeed, sex and magic work in much the same way, beginning with a desire, expending energy to raise power and momentum, followed by the climax and release.

In magic the desire is the visualized outcome of the spell – that is, what you want to happen or bring into being. Raising the power can be done in any number of ways, including chanting an incantation, drumming, dancing or singing. The power is released as the practitioner lights the candle, burns the spell paper, stops chanting, and then opens the magic circle.

In sex the desire is the attraction to another individual, that first spark of recognition that here is someone you really like. The energy expended is that of sexual arousal and the act of intercourse itself. The release is obviously the point of orgasm. With such close parallels between the two activities it should come as no surprise to learn that witches sometimes use the force of sex and orgasm to add power to their rituals. They do this by focusing on their magical goal and by visualizing its positive outcome during the act of sex. Orgasm then releases the magical power and the goal goes out into the universe. Successful sex magic in this sense depends on both partners visualizing the same goal and maintaining a strong, focused visualization throughout love making. This is easier said than done, but maintaining focus is vital if you want your sex ritual to be effective. Although a simultaneous orgasm is not essential, if one of you arrives at climax when the other one has barely even taken off, it could have a detrimental effect on the spell's manifestation. So if you want to give couple's sex magic a go and your partner is willing, here are a few things for you to bear in mind:

- Decide upon your chosen goal and agree that you will both focus on its positive manifestation.
- Try to arrive at the point of orgasm as close together as you possibly can; so if you know it takes longer for you to get revved up, plan lots of foreplay prior to intercourse.
- Set the scene with incense, candles, pretty lingerie and sumptuous bed linen.
- Have a boudoir feast all prepared, ready to ground your energies after the ritual.
- Finally cast a protective circle around the bed or your area of choice to keep the power free of any negative vibes. There are many ways to do this. Try walking around the bed and sprinkling red and pink rose petals as you go, or cast a visionary circle by imagining the bed within a circle of fire or a warm pink bubble. Casting a circle is a visionary exercise, but you should both agree upon the visualization. Cast the circle together or let one of you sit in bed while the other casts the circle around it. As you cast say, 'I cast this sacred circle of love!' When the circle is complete join your lover in bed and let the magic begin. Be sure to take up the petals and bury them in the garden, or imagine your visionary circle is fading away, once your magic is over. Now enjoy the boudoir feast to ground and replenish your energies and know that your magical power has gone out into the universe to do your bidding.

## Solitary Sex Magic

There might be a time you are without a partner, or your lover refuses to take part in a sex magic ritual – that is his prerogative and no one should feel under pressure to perform in this way. In such a situation you will have to do it alone. Whether you decide to use sex toys or choose to let your fingers do the walking, all the same rules apply as with couple's sex magic, so set the scene and cast the circle of your choice. Although you will not need to concern yourself with anyone else's sex patterns and climax rate, you will still need to maintain a strong visualization of your magical goal. At the moment of your orgasm concentrate really hard on your goal. Be completely single-minded in your ritual desire. Once your magic is over and you have taken down the circle to release the magic you have created, eat your boudoir feast to ground and replenish your energy.

*Successful sex magic depends on a steady build-up of energy and power so take your time and do not rush to orgasm. The longer the whole thing takes the more power you will build, so if your man is driving you wild five minutes into it, ask him to take it down a notch or two. Likewise if you know that sex toys bring you to frenzy within seconds, then leave them to one side.*

CHAPTER 4

# Glamour Girl

The perfect temptress is always perfectly groomed; her hair shines, her skin glows, her nails are neatly manicured and expertly polished. A waft of deliciously fine fragrance lingers in the air as she moves from room to room and goes about her busy day. Each morning, as she prepares for the day ahead she chooses to wear beautiful lingerie, a lovely outfit and complementary shoes. She accessorizes with care, adorning her best features with appropriate jewellery, without going so over the top that she begins to resemble a Yuletide tree! Her look is always refined, sophisticated and understated; the word 'bling' is not in her vocabulary, and it certainly does not feature in her wardrobe.

At the weekend or during her time off from work she will indulge herself with breakfast in bed, long soaks in a bubbly bath, lunch with friends and maybe even a shopping spree for girly trifles. After completing the daily chores that we all have to contend with and make time for, a smart temptress will make time for herself, relaxing in her boudoir flipping through a pile of fashion magazines. She might enjoy a romantic dinner with her beau, or share a bottle of wine and a good gossip with her girlfriends.

Of course there will be days when even a Wiccan temptress feels less than stellar. In this case the last thing she may want to do is get dressed up to the nines or take part in sexual Olympics! Even a temptress needs a day off now and then, but if she is relaxing at home nursing a cold, reading a good book or watching a fabulous new film, she makes the effort to cosy up in an elegant lounge suit or a beautiful pair of satin pyjamas and matching slippers. Can you imagine anything more glamorous and indulgent than spending the day in a lovely silk kimono sipping luxury hot chocolate or a glass of wine and nibbling on a selection of tasty treats as you watch your favourite old movies? Greta Garbo had the right idea – sometimes a girl just wants to be alone!

An elegant kimono, kaftan or pair of satin pyjamas should be at the top of every girl's shopping list, while a decadent 'pj day' should be factored into her schedule on a regular basis; not only will this help her to recharge her batteries after a strenuous working week, but it will pander to her inner siren and leave her feeling positively A-list. Take a leaf out of Mariah Carey's book; she claims that when she is at home alone she rarely wears clothes but instead pads around her apartment in sexy kaftans, silk teddies and cami sets. If such glamorous behaviour is good enough for her then it is certainly one aspect of celebrity lifestyle worth imitating!

##  The Glamorous Life

The archetype of the Wiccan temptress advocates a glamorous lifestyle, but this does not necessarily mean that you need to be a Lotto winner to connect with your inner seductress and live a life of glamour. Often it is the simple things that can make a big difference, and discovering the romance in the mundane is the best way to beautify daily life. So although expensive beauty treatments are very nice they are not essential. You can quite easily mix up some fabulous beauty potions in your own kitchen, which will have the advantage of a magical twist! A long, soothing scented bubble bath will leave you feeling far more pampered than a quick shower, and it has the added advantage that you can soak in a magical blend of essential oils. Wearing a satin eye mask to bed will make you feel like a film star and will help you to get enough beauty sleep during the lighter brighter months of summer. And applying a home-made face pack before reclining to listen to soothing music or to read a book of erotic fantasy fiction will leave you positively glowing – in more ways than one!

Of course you do not need to change your whole life to make yourself feel like a temptress; just make a few small adjustments to increase the glamour in your daily life. In this way romance and glamour will fit easily into your current commitments and lifestyle and your daily life will be greatly enhanced. Many women are relentlessly juggling family, career, relationships and home making, which can lead to acute stress, so it is essential that you take the opportunity to pamper yourself. Everyone is entitled to a little 'me-time', and when you make the effort to dedicate it to your inner temptress and all the glamour she craves, you will feel twice as sexy and womanly.

## Do Not Worship False Images

Although the media would have us believe that glamour depends on a stick thin figure, a pre-cancerous sun-tan, and so much lip collagen one could easily be mistaken for a kissing gourami when in the pool, real glamour shines from the inside out; it does not necessarily involve superficial modifications. We all know that we should not be influenced by such images, yet most of us have been at some time or another. As intelligent human beings we may know that our only chance of achieving such media perfection would mean going through life in a perpetually air-brushed state, botoxed to the hilt and minus a couple of ribs to ensure the desired waist/hip ratio, but such logic does little to help if you happen to wake up on a 'Fat day'.

If you do find yourself wishing that you could look just like someone on the TV or the catwalk, ask yourself this question: how much of what you see was the media goddess actually born with and how much has been nipped, tucked, sliced, diced, sprayed, dyed, glued, plucked and pouted to *virtual* perfection? This question can help you put the whole illusion, for that is what it is, into some sort of perspective. And while you might never look anything like your favourite celebrity (for you are after all an individual not a clone), at least when you look in the mirror you will know that you are all real and all woman, and you will not be distracted by the imaginary price tags attached to various parts of your anatomy!

It is very irresponsible of the media to advocate such false images of feminine beauty and perfection. Not only does it undermine the confidence of women in general, but it can be very detrimental to the self-image of those people who buy into the illusion. And just imagine the negative effect this bombardment of images is having on young girls. When I was little the Barbie doll was considered to be quite a controversial toy yet, compared with the fashion images around today, she is positively harmless. And in the light of the recent promotion of size zero, Barbie could even be said to be downright porky!

Try to become more aware of how the media manipulate the concept of feminine beauty and do all that you can to shield yourself from their negative effects. That is not to say that you should not make an effort to look good and stay healthy, but try not to compare yourself with false images.

##  Bedazzled by Desire

Desire begins in the mind and the brain is the most erogenous zone of all. In order to be a successful temptress and seductress you must first awaken that spark of desire by being desirable. In short you need to *feel* seductive to *be* seductive. Imagine being at a social event and noticing for the first time a very attractive man. The moment you see him your brain sets to work and you start to think about him. You ask yourself questions such as is he single, is he local, will he notice me, how can I catch his eye? At this point you will probably feel the compelling need to get a closer look at him. You will of course act nonchalantly to let him think that you are completely unaware of his presence! As you apply fresh lip gloss you wonder what it would be like to kiss him. You add a dab of your favourite perfume to ensure that your fragrant calling card will accost his nostrils as you pass him again. Can you see what is happening? You have not even been introduced to the stranger yet, nor are there any guarantees that you will be, but the spark of desire has ignited and your mind is already in seduction mode. And if you are fortunate the stranger may also be having similar thoughts about you too.

Desire begins in the mind. However, successfully transferring it from the brain to the bedroom whilst maintaining its level of intensity can sometimes prove to be quite tricky! Another obstacle to overcome is that we simply never know when or where desire will strike, and it can occasionally catch us unawares. For example, imagine that you have popped out to the shop on a Sunday morning for a loaf of bread or a newspaper wearing a grubby old track suit. Your hair is pulled back into a quick-fix pony tail and you are the picture of domestic drudgery without the merest hint of perfume or lip gloss about your person. This is when you bump headlong into a gorgeously turned out man. The fact that this earth-bound god barely gives you a second glance is perfectly humiliating. This does not mean that you are anything less than gorgeous or that you are not a great catch; it simply means that on that particular morning your outfit and appearance did nothing to push a particular man's love buttons or ignite the desire in his mind and so he passed you by.

Now imagine that this same man saw you out running wearing a sexy hot-pink jogging ensemble. Your hair is bouncing with health, your cheeks are glowing and your lips gleam with a juicy gloss. How could he help but notice you? Or perhaps he bumps into you as you buy fresh flowers for your home. You are wearing a floaty feminine dress and pretty sandals and you bury your nose in the petals to breathe in the fragrant blooms, your eyes closed with pleasure at their scent. How different might his reaction be? And how much more likely is it that he would say good morning and perhaps start chatting, or at the very least throw you his most charming smile?

Now I am by no means saying that you should live your life around the possibility of attracting a man, or that capturing masculine attention should be your sole mission. I have already said that being a temptress does not depend on having a man in your life – or indeed, having one present at all! What I am saying is that it pays to be prepared. A smart temptress would never leave the house without first checking her appearance in a mirror and at the very least running a brush through her hair and applying lip gloss. You should always take steps to be desirable and gorgeous, for your own sake as much as anyone else's; you will probably feel much better about yourself in general if you have taken steps to look good. And if you cannot seduce yourself into feeling desirable, then you will have little hope of seducing anyone else into feeling desire for you. Moreover, you never know who you might meet in a day: an old flame, an ex-boyfriend, an old rival girlfriend maybe. By making sure that you are always well turned out you will feel better prepared to meet and greet whomever and whatever the day has in store for you. Of course the Wiccan temptress adds a touch of magic to her natural allure, but the spells and rituals will not hide greasy hair, scuffed shoes or chipped nail polish, nor can magic replace the merits of basic self-presentation.

## Temptress Tip

*Hang a mirror in the hall or near the main entrance to your home. Nearby keep a hair brush, lip gloss, a bottle of perfume and a decent pair of shoes, and use them each time you leave the house. You will soon look and feel like a glamour girl, even when you take out the bin!*

## Gorgeously Groomed

A woman who takes good care of herself is always infinitely more attractive and desirable than one who does not. There is no greater crime against the inner siren than letting yourself go. These days everyone can afford to buy a bar of soap, a tube of toothpaste, a bottle of shampoo and a deodorant, yet if you take a look around any city centre or venture on to public transport, you will see people who obviously would not recognize a shower-head if it hit them in the face! A lack of regard towards personal hygiene is an insult to society and to those of us who do make an effort.

Personal presentation should be second nature. We are not living in the Middle Ages and it is never acceptable to look (or smell) as though you have been dragged through a hedge backwards. And of course, looking sexy will make you feel sexy and this in turn can increase your self-confidence and self-esteem.

Like most women I dress for myself, not for anyone else; I adore clothes and fashion. I think that most women would agree that they too dress for themselves first and for their man second. When a woman is out shopping she buys the items that *she* likes, and if her partner happens to like them too then that is an added bonus.

One common complaint made against men is that when buying clothes or lingerie for their partner, they invariably choose the sexiest thing in the shop, with little regard for their partner's age, body shape or personal taste. Perhaps this is the reason that many women have to fight their way through the January Sale crowds in order to take back a gift. What a man deems to be sexy is not necessarily what makes a woman *feel* sexy. Having said that, a thoughtful gift of tasteful lingerie can often be the start of a great night in; the emphasis though is on tasteful! This tendency on the part of men to go for the sexiest item on display probably has something to do with their love trigger; a man's sexuality is stimulated by visual cues and he gets turned on by what he sees. Women tend to be more tactile and emotional in their sexuality, so their cues come from how something makes them feel. So while a rubber Basque with bondage buckles might look great to some men, a woman is more likely to choose a softer one in satin, velvet or lace, with pretty ribbons. This garment is going right next to her skin and so it needs to feel good on if she is to feel good in it. And your lingerie should always match, otherwise you just look thrown together.

So how well do you take care of yourself? A quick visit to your bathroom and dressing table will give you a fairly accurate indication. If you have a preferred range of products neatly lined up in your bathroom, if you have gleaming bath oils, juicy soaps, decadent body lotions, scented candles and a pile of fluffy towels, then you probably spend quite a lot of your time pampering yourself in the bath. If, however, you have a single bar of supermarket soap and a solitary bottle of economy shampoo then you need to introduce yourself to a little luxury as soon as possible. If your dressing table is weighed down with your French perfume bottles and plays host to a well-stocked vanity case of make-up, a manicure set and a box of shimmering body powder with an elegant puff, if the drawers are filled to the brim with sexy, racy lingerie, pretty nightclothes and scented sachets, then you are already a siren and you are well tuned in to your inner goddess. If, however, you do not even own a dressing table or something similar, then you need to get to grips with grooming and set about turning yourself into a siren of seduction!

Basically a temptress takes very good care of every inch of her body, giving herself a weekly check, to keep everything soft, smooth and shipshape. Just when you are presenting yourself to a lover is not the best time to discover that you forgot to shave your legs or than you are wearing your best Bridget Jones knickers! Offering yourself to a lover, even if your have been married for years, is a great gift and as such you should gift wrap yourself accordingly.

So in addition to basic hygiene routines remember to cleanse, tone and moisturize your face and neck. Cleanse twice, as you would when using a shampoo on your hair, the first time to shift surface dirt and dead skin cells and the second time to clean deep into the pores, leaving you with a tingling clean feeling. Make sure that you protect your skin from the sun; wear a lip balm daily to keep your lips kissably soft, and use a hand lotion regularly throughout the day as the hands are usually the first body part to show signs of ageing. Use a facial night cream each evening before going to bed and lavish on body lotion directly after every bath or shower you take to keep your skin supple and moisturized, and to leave it feeling like satin. Use a shine serum on your hair for added gleam and whitening toothpaste to make your smile radiant. Also think about using a body scrub, hair rinse, face steam and face pack once every week. At the same time manicure your hands and pedicure your feet. Pluck your eyebrows and wax or shave as necessary.

While this routine might sound like a lot to do, it is really very easy and you probably do half of it already anyway. It will keep your skin, hair and nails in tiptop condition and being comfortable in your own skin is so much easier if your skin feels like satin. You do not need to spend a lot of money on products if you do not want to; while expensive creams are nice to have, a basic baby lotion works fantastically well if you are strapped for cash. Alternatively, get the ingredients needed to make your own products on your next visit to the local supermarket. Discover the magic in the aisles as you browse the herbs, spices and fresh produce! You will find a selection of simple recipes for home-made beauty potions at the end of this chapter to whet your appetite.

Once your body is pampered and at its very best wrap it in beautiful matching lingerie, sprinkle it with an intoxicating French perfume, smear a touch of gloss on your lips, tousle your hair and *voilà*!

*Devise a beauty routine that fits in with your daily schedule and make full use of your preferred products and potions. Pamper yourself thoroughly at least once a week to maintain your glamour and allure!*

##  Personal Presentation

All your hard work so far will be in vain if your outfit lets you down. While this book is not about fashion, the basic wardrobe of a temptress needs to be addressed, if only to save some women from making the mistake of thinking that nearly naked is the new black! Being seductive does not mean dressing in a tarty, trashy way. Quite the contrary in fact, for a good temptress knows that it is the suggestion of what is underneath the clothing which is far sexier than having it all out on display to the universe! Once again, think of dressing as gift wrapping yourself and conceal more than you reveal. Keep him guessing. The suggestion of a cleavage is far sexier than a top which is too low cut and leaves nothing to the imagination. If you think that covering up will work against you, think again; men love a challenge and if you make things too easy for them they will despise you for it. They might well sleep with you, they might even string you along for a while, but they won't respect you very much or treat you as you deserve.

When it comes to sophisticated, seductive dressing there is one golden rule: draw attention to only one half of the body at a time. So, if you are wearing a miniskirt or a pair of hotpants, wear a high-necked, long-sleeved top to give you a very sexy silhouette. If you are wearing a cropped, strapless or shoulderless top, wearing a long skirt, trousers or even smart jeans will bring elegance to your ensemble. The trick is to show just enough skin to make him long to see more!

Remember also that a good temptress has her own style; she does not slavishly follow fashion – why would she want to look just like everyone else? This ability to turn heads and stand out from the crowd without resorting to outrageous dress or bad behaviour is what helps to make a temptress attractive. Elegance and sophistication are her watchwords. She knows that style is more artistic and more lasting than fashion, style can be worn with more flair, style does not depend on size and shape, style can turn heads and set tongues wagging for all the right reasons. So begin to develop a signature style for yourself and learn how to stand out from the crowd in an elegant and dignified manner. Self-respect will make you sexier than ever, and as you develop your personal esteem and individuality your natural sex appeal will turn far more heads than a barely-there dress. Finally make sure you have the following staples of the temptress's wardrobe:

- A little back dress or LBD
- A little red dress or LRD
- A wrap-over dress
- A feminine floaty dress
- Black trousers which enhance the *derrière*
- A black roll-neck top
- A slim-fitting, calf-length black skirt
- A white shirt
- A great pair of heels
- A pair of pretty sandals
- A great pair of knee boots

If you have all of these basics in your wardrobe you can dress them up or down, and mix and match with other items, depending on the season and occasion, but you will always look sexy, slinky and sophisticated.

## How to Talk a Man into Bed

The most seductive organ of all is the human brain. Interesting people are rarely lonely and the intellect is a woman's strongest weapon of seduction, particularly when good conversation is generously sprinkled with sparkling wit. Men love intelligent women, largely I think because the bimbo image has been done to death and is just as insulting to men as it is to woman – what intelligent man would want to spend time with a bimbo?

A relationship of any kind usually begins with a meeting of minds. The physical aspects generally come later. I am not talking about one-night stands, which are a recreational quick fix, but a genuine relationship built to last. Couples spend many hours getting to know one another in the first stages of their relationship. It is during this early stage that similarities are explored and celebrated, and complementary differences are a source of great rejoicing (uncomplementary differences tend to be swiftly glossed over, until they come back to haunt you at a later date). A healthy and lasting relationship depends upon good communication and on the couple's ability to talk through problems and differences without being disrespectful to one another, even when they disagree. The success of any relationship depends on the lines of honest and respectful communication staying open. Once you stop talking to each other, or worse still stop listening to each other, the relationship is in trouble.

We have seen how desire begins in the mind. The first spark of attraction is lit within the brain, and when the introductions are made you need to be ready! It is quite possible to talk a man into bed, and equally possible to be talked into bed by a man. So why are women surprised when they wake up next to the man they were chatting with all night? Good conversation is mental foreplay, and like all good foreplay, when the right buttons are being consistently pressed by someone you like the resulting climax is virtually inevitable.

This verbal foreplay and meeting of minds is essential if the relationship is going to progress. There is nothing more disheartening then being chatted up by a gorgeous man who also happens to be a perfect bore. Likewise men tend to fall in love with women who have brains as well as natural beauty. A great seductress is fully aware of this fact and makes sure that she has interesting things to say through her scarlet lips. She hones her wit and sharpens her intellect with current events programmes, extensive reading and openness to new experiences. She absorbs culture like a sponge and can hold up her end of any conversation. She knows that the more information she absorbs the more interesting her conversation will be and therefore the more absorbed and enraptured her partner will be.

First impressions do count, so when you enter into a conversation with someone make an effort to sound intelligent and listen twice as much as you talk. When you are trying to seduce a man this is especially important; he will not make the moves unless you pause for breath! Listen to what he has to say and make him feel that he is the most fascinating man you have ever met in your life. Do this in a dignified manner though; do not fawn all over him. Ask several intelligent questions to draw him out even more, but do not turn it into an interrogation.

When the conversation turns, as all good conversations do, and he asks about you, make sure you have something interesting to say. Tell him about a play or a ballet you saw recently, or the book you are reading, or an interesting aspect of your job. Discuss where you both stand on the political debate of the moment – and there is always one, otherwise politicians would not have jobs! Now is the time to make him believe that you are the most fascinating, captivating woman in the whole room; make him believe that he has never met anyone quite like you, which if you play up to your strengths, will be nothing short of the absolute truth. This technique is not just for new couples either; in fact it is probably even more important for married and long-term lovers to continue to find one another interesting and surprising. To put it in the simplest of terms, if you make the conversation interesting, then you have a much better chance of making a successful seduction later on, for you will have courted his mind and captured his imagination.

## Beauty Lotions and Potions

We end this chapter with a selection of easy-to-prepare beauty potions which you can whip up in the kitchen, making full use of natural ingredients and the gifts of the Goddess. Such natural pampering will help you to make the most of what you have, as nothing is more beautifying to a woman than the gifts of Mother Nature.

### *Sexy Skin Body Scrub*

Mix together two tablespoons of rolled oats, two tablespoons of desiccated coconut and one tablespoon of fine sea salt. Stir them well and then add two teaspoons of golden honey and enough double cream to form a paste. Use the body scrub all over, rubbing it in to slough off dead skin. Work in circular motions, moving towards the heart to stimulate circulation. Shower off with cool water to close the pores, then apply your favourite body lotion to leave you skin with a sexy, polished glow.

### *Horse Chestnut Hair Rinse*

On a bright summer day gather a small pan of horse chestnut leaves. Wash them well under a cold tap, then place them in a large pan of spring water and bring to the boil. Once boiling, turn down the heat and allow the leaves to simmer for ten to fifteen minutes. Strain the water into a large bowl and put the leaves out onto the compost heap or leave them in a corner of the garden, thus giving them back to nature. Allow the hair rinse to cool until it is tepid, then after shampooing, use a jug to pour the rinse over your hair again and again, catching it in the sink or bowl. Once your hair has been thoroughly drenched in the rinse, towel dry and style as usual. Your hair will be soft and shiny. Throw the rest of the rinse down the drain, offering up words of thanks to the Goddess.

### *Floral Facial Steam*

Pour hot, but not boiling water into a large bowl and add the following pure essential oils: two drops of geranium, two drops of ylang ylang and one drop of lavender. Tie your hair back and lean over the bowl, covering your head with a towel. Steam your face for about twenty minutes to draw out any impurities and clean deep into the pores of the skin. Afterwards pat your face dry and throw the steam potion away. Then apply the face pack below.

## Refreshing Face Pack

Take half a cucumber, slice it and grind it to a mush. Add two teaspoons of golden honey and mix to a paste. Apply the face pack to face and neck and relax for about twenty minutes to half an hour. Your skin will be refreshed by the cucumber, and the honey will help to keep your complexion soft and smooth. Rinse off with tepid water until your face and neck are completely clean, then pat dry and apply your chosen toner and moisturizer.

## Sexy Bath Blend

For the perfect pre-seduction bath run the water as normal, then just before you step in add two drops each of the following seductive essential oils: ylang ylang, rosewood, cedar wood, geranium, and sandalwood. Lie back and relax, allowing the fine fragrances to waft around you. Give your skin time to absorb the oils and the scent, so stay in the bath for at least half an hour. Towel yourself dry and prepare to seduce!

*As you can see this is all incredibly simple, yet the act of pampering yourself in such a magical way is very effective as you are attuning with the divine feminine via her natural produce, making yourself feel more goddess-like in the process.*

CHAPTER 5

# In My Lady's Chamber

All this pampering of the person will be wasted if your love-nest looks more like a pigsty! A successful temptress always has the perfect backdrop, and her natural habitat is, of course, the boudoir. It is within the sultry walls of the decadent boudoir that the Wiccan temptress can indulge in her passion for glamour and luxury. The boudoir is her refuge, her sanctuary where she can beautify herself, where she can lounge upon the bed in a satin cami set and read racy fiction to rev up her love motor, where she can hide from the world in a face mask on bad days, where she can cast love spells at her goddess altar, and where she can entertain her lover in seductive style.

Creating a boudoir is about setting the scene for love. As soon as you open the door you should hear the siren-call: 'Come in my love and see what pleasures I have in store for you, what wonderful delights await you!' Seduction and romance should be the very first things one thinks of when entering a boudoir – which is far more glamorous and luxurious than a simple bedroom. The boudoir should feel warm and welcoming, inviting and secretive. This is where you and your lover will forget the everyday world and indulge in one another with total abandon; it should feel like stepping into a secret world of romance. It should be cosy and comfortable, and of course it should be sexy but without going over the top. The effect you are trying to achieve is Parisian bordello chic or 1940s film-star glamour, not back-street brothel!

When creating your boudoir imagine that you are the star of the film *Moulin Rouge*. What would you be wearing, what would your signature perfume be, how would you play out the main scene, what would your perfect backdrop be? Now set about recreating a toned down version in your bedroom.

Most women have a very strong nesting instinct, so creating a boudoir should not pose too much of a challenge. Once again, this is not about spending lots of money, but more about introducing subtle touches that lend sex appeal to your sleeping environment. It could be that all your room needs is a coat of paint and a few satin scatter cushions, or a new bed, or a collection of scented candles in pretty holders. Do be aware, however, that the colours you choose and the scents you use to perfume the room can all have an effect on the overall atmosphere and how conducive it is to love and seduction. Also bear in mind that there is nothing less sexy than a computer or work station in the bedroom, piles of dirty laundry, an unmade bed, dirty ashtrays, stained bed linen and a room that is badly in need of a good airing!

## Boudoir Themes

To get your imagination fired up here are some examples of possible themes.

### *Arabian Nights*

An Arabian Nights boudoir is full of Eastern promise. The best colours for this look are deep tones of red, purple, indigo and fuchsia pink. Or opt for more spicy tones such as cinnamon and terracotta with a touch of bronze and gold. Use a low futon-style bed, and tent it in a jewel-coloured bed canopy. Scatter sari cushions on the floor and add a large decorative bong pipe in the corner. Display a figure of an Eastern goddess such as Ishtar or Lakshmi. Burn exotic incense in a brass censer and have candles lit in a collection of Moroccan-style lanterns. Keep an Aladdin's lamp on the windowsill. Play belly-dancing music and seduce your lover with your erotic moves, then feed each other Turkish delight and flip through the pages of the *Karma Sutra*. Release your Eastern princess and free the genie in your lamp!

## Fairy-tale Enchantress

Welcome to *my* boudoir! A fairy-tale boudoir is perfect for those of a romantic turn. Go for a medieval maiden's bedchamber look, using soft colours such as pink, violet and ivory or simple blue and white. Have a four-poster bed as the focal point of the room; the higher this is the better as it will give a 'Princess and the Pea' air to your boudoir. Twine faux vines and briar roses around the bed posts to lend a *Sleeping Beauty* look and keep a crystal glass slipper on the dressing table. Hang an ornate mirror on the wall for your looking-glass moments and hang tapestries on the walls and across the door. Then add sex appeal to the room by hanging Pre-Raphaelite prints of semi-naked sirens and nymphs around the room. Display a statue of a love goddess, for example Aphrodite or Venus. Place vases of fresh roses all around and use rose-scented candles in tall floor-standing candle sticks for that medieval maiden finish. Play harp music and while away the hours with your embroidery as you wait for your knight.

## Moulin Rouge

A deep red background is essential for this boudoir look, so be brave and paint the walls! Use deep burgundy bed linen and lots of velvet scatter cushions. Then hang gilded mirrors, and dot lots of candles in crystal or glass holders all around the room. Burn spicy seductive oil such as ylang ylang or passion flower and have the champagne ready on ice. Add a dressing screen, a chaise longue and bead curtains and you are ready to don your best corset and sing '*Voulez-vous coucher avec moi?*'

### Chocolate

Forget about love; fall in chocolate, the ultimate aphrodisiac! A chocolate-box boudoir is sexy and decadent and just perfect if you live with a man, as it is more subtle than the other styles, and the colours are more neutral so your man might find it easier to live with. Use the colours of a chocolate box so think mocha, coffee, caramel, ivory and chocolate, and add a touch of gold and bronze for more glitz. Soft fabrics such as velvet, faux fur, faux suede and satin will make you want to curl up in it and never leave. Add small round cushions to the bed, keep massage oil in a brown beribboned hatbox by the bed, and always keep a supply of chocolate body-paint on standby! Finishing touches could include chocolates, vanilla and coffee-scented candles, a copy of Joanne Harris's novel *Chocolat* for bedtime reading, a statue of an abundance goddess such as Demeter or Gaia and a small chocolate fountain for those saucy sex games. Forget counting calories, rack up your orgasms!

As you can see from these examples a little imagination goes a long way. But what if you are happy with the bedroom you already have and simply want to sex it up a bit? Here are some tips on spicing up a bedroom without resorting to a complete makeover.

- If you do not have a four-poster bed, then get the look of one using drapes or lace, chiffon or organza. Or buy a readymade bed canopy and drape this over the bed for added glamour.
- Always make sure your bed linen is clean and matching. Pick out pretty pastels or decadent jewel colours. Add scatter cushions and sumptuous throws in soft chenille and faux fur. Make your bed as inviting as possible so that you and your lover enjoy cocooning up here together. Always open a window and air the bedroom daily to keep it fresh and clean.
- If you must have a computer or work station in your bedroom then make sure you can hide it away somehow when it is not in use, either by setting it up in a custom-made cabinet or by using

a decorative screen. Alternatively hang voile or bead curtains from the ceiling to close it off when it is time to indulge in bedroom behaviour.

- Soft lighting is essential in a bedroom and candlelight is by far the most flattering. There is no greater turn-off than a beaming spotlight shining right where you do not want it! So invest in as many beautiful candle holders as you can afford, in different shapes and styles to add variety. Fill the room with scented candles in sexy fragrances such as ylang ylang, vanilla, cinnamon and, the sexiest of all, rose. Light the candles five minutes before you retire to the boudoir to ensure a welcoming fragrance.
- Statues and pictures of sexy loving couples are widely available and you should add one or two to your boudoir to enhance the space and define the purpose of the room – it is not just for sleeping in after all! This is especially true if you are single and looking for love, or if your relationship is going through a tough time, as it will help to bring the essence of love, passion and romance into the bedroom once more.
- Have a small pile of sexy books on display in your boudoir. Keep *The Wiccan Temptress* on your beside table for entertainment and reference. A tasteful collection of lover's guides and erotic fiction will give you and your lover something to flick through as you catch your breath between sex sessions, and the books will also be on hand to put you in the mood on those occasions when your libido might be letting you down.
- Beautiful lingerie need not be hidden away in a drawer; it can help to sex up any bedroom. Use some of your sexy bits and pieces as decorative items by hanging them in plain sight or letting them lie around quite casually. Always use pretty padded hangers to preserve delicate fabrics. Leave a pair of long satin gloves or a feather boa across a chair; throw a chiffon negligée across the end of the bed; hang a pretty nightie from the wardrobe door, or a glamorous robe from the back of the bedroom door. Hang sexy corsets and basques from hooks on

doors and walls, treating them like seductive pictures and create a provocative tableau. I have a pink silk basque hung from the wardrobe door and it adds to the femininity of the room. Using your belongings in this way means that your sexy lingerie is working for you even when you are not wearing it. Choose sexy items in colours that match or co-ordinate with your décor and then scatter them around the room. Your man's imagination will do the rest – but be prepared to model these clothes on request!

- Scent all the lingerie in your drawers by adding floral sachets; you will find recipes for fragrant sachets later in this chapter. Alternatively, the next time you go shopping for a new perfume take home all the fragrance strips you use and add them to your lingerie drawers, handbags and linen closet. In this way all the items in your boudoir will smell like your favourite French fashion house and perfumier!
- Buy a beautiful box or a small chest and place this near to the bed. Then fill it with sensual treats and toys such as massage oils, condoms, flavoured body paints, chocolates, erotic and romantic poetry, feathers, racy gloves and anything else you enjoy. If you have children make sure the box locks, or you will find all your seductive chocolate products gone!
- If you are planning a hot night in with your lover prepare a tray with a few nibbles, finger foods, napkins and chilled wine. Place this in a corner of the bedroom ready for you both to enjoy later on. To increase the romance of this boudoir feast use heart-shaped plates and red napkins and glass ware, which are all available around Valentine's Day, so do stock up then for the year of fun and frolic to come!

## Come Hither Colours

Some colours have a very high sex appeal while others are best left out of the boudoir. Below are the most magically sexy shades.

*Racy red*. Probably the sexiest colour of all for a boudoir, as it shrieks passion and seduction. Bright red may be a little too much, especially if you have trouble sleeping, so choose deep burgundy and claret shades. Lighten the tone with ivory accents or warm it up even more with natural brown shades – think berries and bark, like an elfin grove.

*Provocative pink*. Pink is pure romance, and a fantastic colour for a boudoir. However some men are turned off by a room that is too girly. So use pink with care. Soft rose pinks work well and are a pretty safe bet. Think sophisticated and feminine, but not too girly, so keep well clear of bubble-gum shades; your aim is to turn him on, not make him feel he is playing Ken to your Barbie!

*Tempting violet*. Violet is a more sophisticated alternative to pink and it can be a very sexy colour, particularly when mixed with more vibrant shades of purple and magenta.

*Mystifying blue*. Blue is a great colour for encouraging sleep and relaxation but you will need to accessorize your boudoir very provocatively to lend this colour any kind of sex appeal. A deep midnight blue is probably the sexiest shade to go for if blue is your colour preference. Add some fabulous mirrors and lots of blue velvet to sex it up.

*Monochrome chic*. A feminine black and white room is very sexy and sophisticated indeed and seems to be all the rage at the moment. A boudoir of this style would be positively Parisian. Add pictures of the Eiffel Tower to enhance the look. This combination of black and white is very easy on the male eye too, so your man is likely to feel very comfortable with a boudoir of this choice.

*Colours to avoid*. Orange is just too playschool. Green is so tranquil it could send your lover straight to sleep. Grey will make your boudoir resemble a pair of washed-out old knickers! And there really is nothing sexy about magnolia.

*The boudoir is where the temptress takes centre stage, where the siren-self comes to the fore of your personality, so it is important to get it right particularly if your inner siren is a little shy. Make the stage so inviting that she simply cannot help coming out to flaunt her Goddess-given talents! Create a room so beautiful that your partner can leave all his cares behind, feeling that he has stepped into another world – a world where passion rules and he is free to indulge, for there is nothing that empowers a temptress more than watching a man rise to her bait!*

## Flirtatious Fragrance

Just as different colours lend a different magical energy to a boudoir, fragrances help to change the ambience of a room. The warm scent of vanilla will make it feel very different from one fragranced with the fresh scent of mountain pine. Pure essential oils will always smell much nicer than synthetic air fresheners, and because the oils come from nature and Mother Earth they can be used in your Wiccan magic too.

Witches tend to fragrance their homes every day as they burn scented candles for a spell working, or incense for banishing and protection rituals. In addition we might burn oils to bring about a specific magical goal – for example, we might burn rose oil to bring love into the house, or we might use fragrance to honour a sabbat or a season, or to create a specific atmosphere, say for example burning cinnamon and clove to make a room more inviting to Yuletide guests.

Scents stay with us for a long time, and they can evoke powerful memories. Think about the scent of baking bread, freshly ground coffee, the Sunday roast, chocolate, the tang of the sea breeze, the smoky air of bonfire night. These are all very different fragrances which can evoke different memories and moods.

Using fragrance in the boudoir, or indeed your whole house, can help you to achieve a very specific ambience, and there are many different ways in which you can use fragrance. I have already mentioned scented candles, but you might also like to try burning incense sticks or cones, or use an oil burner to heat essential oils – fill the well with hot water, sprinkle on a few drops of oil and light the tea-light underneath. As the candle heats the water the fragrance of the oil is slowly released, filling the room with scent. Fresh flowers are another fantastic way to add scent to a boudoir; red roses are my personal favourite, romantic that I am! Or you could make your own room sprays with essential oil blends. To get you started with the vast world of romantic fragrance here is a list of some of the most magically appropriate scents for a boudoir – some of which are said to have aphrodisiac qualities.

*Rose*. The ultimate in sexy, romantic fragrance. Use in any format: oils, candles, pot pourri or fresh flowers, and use with abandon! The scent of roses will turn your boudoir into a romantic haven, a fragrant rose-bower. It is ideal for the spring and summer months.

*Geranium*. This is a very feminine scent, and it can have an uplifting effect, so burn geranium oil when you need your boudoir to be more of a private retreat. Shut the world out and breathe in the scent. It is also said to be an aphrodisiac which works well on the female libido.

*Ylang ylang*. This oil is reputed to be something of an aphrodisiac too; it certainly seems to have an effect on the male libido. It is the best scent to use when you plan to seduce your lover. The essential oil can be added to a massage blend to give a powerful boost to your intimate moments together. So if you are planning a hot night in, begin by running a bath scented with about eight drops of ylang ylang oil. Then bathe together in bliss! Ylang ylang oil is powerful stuff and it can help to kick start virtually anyone's love motor! Bear this in mind if your love life needs a boost.

*Lavender*. The scent of lavender is not to everyone's taste, so use it sparingly. In the boudoir it is best used as a spray to scent your bed linen, cushions and curtains. It has a calming and healing effect, so its fragrance will help you nod off to sleep or enjoy an afternoon nap. It is fantastic when you are in bed nursing the flu, and it is also an excellent moth repellent.

*Vanilla*. The warm fragrance of vanilla can turn your boudoir into a cosy retreat on dark winter nights. It has rather a woody scent, reminiscent of an autumnal forest. Use it with wild, elfin abandon all through the autumn and winter months. On cold nights scent extra rugs and faux fur throws with a drop or two of vanilla oil and cocoon beneath the covers with your lover. If you have a real fire try throwing one or two vanilla pods on the coals to create a woodland retreat in your own home. Many bath and body products are available with a vanilla scent, so treat yourself to a selection of these and you will not only smell quite delicious, your skin will be as smooth as silk too.

*Cinnamon*. This is another great fragrance for winter, especially during the Yuletide season, so if you are planning some festive flirtations scent your boudoir with cinnamon, mull some wine and hang a bough of mistletoe from your bed post – the perfect Yuletide romantic retreat.

*Perfume*. If you are pushed for time, or simply feeling extravagant, then spray some of your favourite French perfume on to cotton balls and tuck them behind the radiators. This will quickly fill your boudoir with a gorgeous fragrance. Can anything be more glamorous than a boudoir which smells of Chanel or Dior?

*Pine*. Pine is not a very sexy fragrance, but it does have its uses. It has powerful cleansing properties, and so magically speaking it is perfect for banishing bad-boyfriend vibes and negative bedroom karma. Burn pine incense if your relationship is going through a bad patch, if you have recently broken up with someone or if you cannot remember your last orgasm.

## Enticing Blends

If you have a small collection of pure essential oils then you can have lots of fun witching up your own boudoir blends to fragrance your room, linen and throws. This has the advantage that you know exactly what is going into your blends, unlike the ones you might purchase from a shop. Also you can imbue them with magic as you make them. What is more this type of witchery is incredibly easy; all you need are a collection of pure essential oils, spring water (the bottled variety is just fine) clean spritzer bottles in which to store your blends, and sticky labels with which to identify them. Experiment with various fragrances and combinations, as fragrance is very much a personal preference. Here are some basic recipes to get you started. As you make each blend, strongly visualize the effect you want it to have to add the magic to the mix.

*Romance blend*. Add five drops of rosewood, three drops of rose-geranium and two drops of foxglove oil to 100ml of pure spring water. Pour into a spritzer bottle and label. Shake well before use and use as a room and linen spray.

*Wildwood blend*. Add two drops each of the following essential oils to 100ml of spring water: fern, oak moss, foxglove, bluebell and lavender. Shake well and use daily, and when ironing bed linen.

*Sensual blend*. Add three drops each of ylang ylang, rose-geranium and cedarwood to 100ml of pure spring water. Shake well and use as a room and linen spray.

*Massage blend for her*. Make a seductive and feminine massage blend for your lover to use on you by choosing flirty fragrances of rose-geranium, African violet and jasmine oils. Add two drops of each essential oil to 10ml of carrier such as sweet almond oil. Mix well and store in a clean dark glass blending bottle.

*Massage blend for him*. Seduce your man by giving him a long sensual massage using the following home-made massage blend: add two drops each of ylang ylang, sandalwood and frankincense essential oils to 10ml of carrier such as sweet almond or jojoba oil. Mix well and store in a clean dark glass blending bottle.

## Scented Sachets

Fragrant sachets have been used for centuries as a way of delicately scenting clothes and linen. Although they can be bought in shops they are easy enough to make at home. Choose some pretty fabric and sew it into small pouches or heart shapes. Stuff the pouches with your favourite floral blend (see below) and sew the final part together. Alternatively cut the fabric into squares, add some of the floral blend to the centre of the square, then gather the fabric up and tie it tightly with a pretty ribbon. Refresh the sachets with new floral blends or a few drops of essential oil. Scatter the sachets around your home: place them in drawers, stationery pigeon holes, wardrobes, cloak rooms, linen closets, blanket chest, towel bales, suitcases, etc. Here are two simple blends to get you started.

*Floral blend*. Mix together two tablespoons of dried rose petals, one tablespoon of dried lavender and one tablespoon of dried camomile. Use this blend in your sachets and as a finishing touch sprinkle each sachet with a couple of drops of rose-geranium oil.

*Herbal blend*. Mix together two tablespoons of dried lavender, one tablespoon of dried rosemary, and one tablespoon of dried thyme and use this blend in your sachets. Sprinkle the sachets with a couple of drops of cedarwood oil. This herbal woody blend is perfect for keeping moths at bay, so store these sachets with out of season clothes, in suitcases, linen closets, cloak rooms, etc.

## Boudoir Behaviour

Aside from herbal witchery, what exactly does a temptress get up to in her boudoir? Men have been pondering on this question for some time and Peter Sarstedt actually wrote a song about it, crooning out the lyrics 'Where do you go to my lovely, when you're alone in your bed?' There is a cloak of mystery that surrounds what women do in their bedrooms. Why do we spend so much time in there, why does it take us so long to prepare for a big night out? What are we doing?

The boudoir is a woman's sanctuary. It is the place where she prepares to face the world, applying make-up and picking out her outfit, trying on the perfect ensemble. It is where she gets intimate with her partner, or even with herself! It is where she rests and recharges her batteries, where she can close the door, shutting out the rest of the world. Ultimately the boudoir is where a woman can be totally and completely herself. Following a bad day at work or a disagreement with a spouse, women tend to take refuge in the bedroom. And even if this room is shared between a married or co-habiting couple, it is still very much *her* space.

My boudoir has always been a very personal and private space. Even when I was a young girl I would spend time in my bedroom after school, absorbing the feminine pinkness of it all after the jarring atmosphere of the classroom. I still spend a lot of time in my boudoir and I guard the privacy of this space jealously; when I am in here, the world does not exist. Of all the rooms in my house the boudoir is where the vulnerable side of my personality becomes apparent – only I and the people whom I trust implicitly are allowed in this room, so I am free to express any vulnerability I might have. The softer, romantic aspects of my character which I generally keep hidden from the outside world are on full display in my bedroom. Here I am surrounded by knights in armour gazing down at me from the walls as I lie on the four-poster bed, or sit on the chaise longue reading poetry or stitching tapestries; the fragrance of roses permeates the air and burning candles cast flickering shadows around the room. This is my personal fantasy space, where I can be who I really am, without wearing a mask or putting on the Ice Maiden persona which gets me through the trials of daily life. When I am in my bedroom, all the hats I usually wear fall off; I am not a writer working on her latest book, I am not an author promoting her work, I am not a daughter, sister, or friend worrying that I might disappoint someone, I am not trying to live up to expectations, perceptions or deadlines; in my boudoir I am simply Marie – no more, no less, just me.

This is the kind of space and freedom which a lovely boudoir can offer a woman. Whatever her career or personal circumstances, here in her fantasy room, she can gain some much-needed peace and mental freedom. She can close the door on family life, forget about her career for a while. Most importantly she can relax into herself for an hour or so, for it is only when you are truly happy with yourself that you can be happy with someone else.

## *Indulge Yourself*

One of the best ways to indulge your inner temptress is to spend a day in her natural environment and be the belle of the boudoir. This is a lovely way to spend a day off from work, to hide away on a rainy day, or just to enjoy a little much-needed 'me-time'. And so long as you have made a few simple preparations, a day in your room will be far from boring; it will leave you relaxed and fully recharged. There are many things that you can enjoy doing in your boudoir. Try out some of the spells and rituals in this book for a start. Experiment with new hair styles and make-up techniques, giving yourself a bit of a make-over – if you are not going to go anywhere it will not matter if you mess it up, and the practice will be worth it when you do go out. Flip through fashion magazines or read inspirational books as you nibble your favourite luxury chocolates. Make a start on writing your own novel or poem. Read the latest bestseller or a racy bodice-ripper. Set up a lover goddess altar (which we will be exploring later on in the book). Put on your favourite music and dance provocatively on the bed.

Make sure that your boudoir is a pleasant environment to be in all day. Throw open a window so that you can feel the spring breeze or hear the birds sing. If it is cold out make full use of fluffy throws and hot chocolate drinks. Following your morning shower put on a glamorous nightdress and negligée, then enjoy a continental breakfast in bed, complete with fresh croissants and cherry compote. Do some yoga, dance or stretching exercises. Fluff up the pillows and read a great book. Fragrance the room with your home-made floral blends, light scented candles and listen to soothing music as you pluck your eyebrows, use a face pack and paint your nails. Ensure that you have all your favourite things to eat and perform the blessing of the boudoir feast which appears later in this chapter. Meditate, have a power nap, write in your diary, chat to friends and family on the phone. Watch an old movie; I enjoy nothing more than a fantasy fling with Errol Flynn in my boudoir on a rainy afternoon! At the end of the day order your favourite take out meal for dinner, pour a glass of wine and invite a lover over for even more indulgence. After a day of indulging yourself it is nice to let someone else indulge you too!

## Temptress Under Fire

In every woman's life there will be days when she is feeling less than stellar. During times of stress or sadness we need a place where we can lick our wounds, cry our sorrows away and prepare ourselves to come out fighting fit once more. On such occasions the boudoir really does become a retreat. Every woman is entitled to a little 'me-time', regardless of how lengthy her to-do list might be. No matter what demands your family or career place upon you, you will be far more capable if you take a little time out. However, 'me-time' is something which you must take, not wait to be given, as you could be waiting a very long time!

I believe that colds, flu, migraines and PMT are the body's way of telling us to slow down a little and take things easy for a day or two. Many women suffer quite badly from PMT and just want to be left alone. When the daily routine prevents them from having time and space to themselves they become irritable, snappy and angry.

The menopause can have similar effects, and the post-baby blues can throw some women into a deep depression. On such occasions the inner temptress tends to fall into the background, the libido takes a holiday and glamour is something other women have. But like charity, tender loving care begins at home. So when you are feeling under the weather, for whatever reason, take good care of yourself and retreat into your boudoir. Take a hot-water bottle and a throw for comfort, take the cat for company, sip a warm drink and just relax. Indulge your emotions with a great film. If you are feeling weepy then put on a sad film and cry it all out. If you are more like me and feel as if you could cheerfully rip someone's head off, put on a film that indulges your warrior princess. I like *Braveheart, Boudicca, Kingdom of Heaven, Troy* and *Gladiator* for those days. This kind of vicarious violence really does help – there is nothing that heals my PMT better than watching a few heads roll!

## Satisfaction Guaranteed

A great temptress never fakes an orgasm because she never needs to. Nor does she indulge herself in petty jealousies or worry that her man will cheat on her. If he is going to cheat then he does not deserve her attentions anyway and she is better off without him.

The temptress is confident in her ability to please a man and she knows her own body so well that she experiences great pleasure when sharing it with her lucky lover. It always amazes me when women claim to be faking their orgasms and then wonder why they are feeling insecure about their relationships. There is no greater insult to a man than to fake your orgasm when you have sex with him. You may think that he does not know, but he probably suspects. You might be making all the rights noises and putting on a show, but the fact is that the vital signs will be missing. When a woman reaches her climax a rush of blood sends a subtle flush to her face, neck and chest. At the same time her nipples harden and the vaginal walls contract. So some things just can't be faked.

Most women expect fidelity from their men, and it is within their power to make ensuring it much easier! If the sex is great, if he knows that he can give you the best orgasms of your life, if such pleasures are reciprocated and he also has the thrill of removing your sexy lingerie every night of the week, then why would he stray? On the other hand, if he knows or suspects that you fake your orgasms, or that you do not enjoy making love with him, if he sees only the same old washed out underwear day in and day out, if you make no effort to please him or meet his sexual needs, then why would he stay? He is far more likely to move on to a woman who does enjoy herself in the bedroom. Men do not want a woman who fakes it; they want a woman who enjoys and who is satisfied by sex just as much as they are. Knowing that they are pressing all the right buttons and turning you on is what turns them on.

The best way to avoid faking orgasms is to know exactly what you like, where you like it and how you like it. How can you expect a man to press the right buttons if you yourself do not know where they are or how they like to be worked? And I am not just talking about the obvious areas – you need to get to know your body as a whole, and one of the ways you can do that is by finger tracing.

## Finger Tracing

Go to your boudoir and make sure that you will not be disturbed. Take off all your clothes and sit naked on the bed. Now lightly trace your fingers all over your body, beginning at your feet and ankles and moving upwards from there. Take notice of what feels good, where you are ticklish and where the slightest touch really turns you on. Continue in this manner until you are acquainted with all your erogenous zones and until you feel that you know your body extremely well. Then move on to the next stage.

## Through the Looking-glass

Next use a hand mirror to look at your genitalia; this is the very core of your womanhood and you should know how it appears to your lover. Most men have an intimate, almost romantic, emotional bond with their penis, and I believe that women could benefit from developing a similar relationship with their vaginas. This is after all where new life can be created, so it is a part of your goddess-centre and a very sacred place. Now get to know yourself intimately and make a mental note of what you are doing that feels good so that you can share this information with your lover. The clitoris is the female nerve centre; it is the place where all your orgasms are stored up just waiting to be released. And unlike a woman's fertile eggs, she can never run out of orgasms; alcohol may only enhance them and she does not stop producing them beyond a certain age!

## The Sex Factor

Once you have got to know yourself in this intimate way you will be able to share your wisdom with your man – in a way that is sensitive to his feelings of course. Try guiding his hand until he hits the spot. Or if you are shy, wait until he accidentally hits the spot and let out a well-timed gasp, then tell him it feels good. This can work wonders! Better still, let him watch you masturbate so that he can make his own mental notes and see exactly what it is that brings you to a hip-writhing climax. This will really turn him on, so prepare to be ravished afterwards!

Faking orgasms on a regular basis is not conducive to a happy, fulfilling relationship as you are basically reinforcing the wrong bedroom moves for your body. Every woman is different, what turns one on might leave another cold. Rather than accepting a bad lot and faking it, you should be asking for and helping him to make all the right moves instead. So if you have been in a relationship for several years and have never had a genuine orgasm then the fault lies with you just as much as with your partner. Do something about it! Get proactive, get to know yourself so that your man can get to know you even better. If you repeat the above exercises regularly then you should never have to fake another orgasm.

##  Boudoir Banquet

Enjoying great sex can work up an appetite, and certain foods can work up an appetite for more sex. Sharing food is an ancient hospitality custom and it is steeped in folklore. Many foods are considered to be aphrodisiacs, as they are said to bring about a heightened state of sexual arousal and can leave one feeling erotically charged. Others, chocolate for example, release the same feel-good hormones that an orgasm does, and so can leave one feeling very satisfied indeed.

Enjoying a boudoir feast is the height of decadence and, providing you put a little thought and effort into it, there is no need for it to be regarded as slobbish. Even the elegant courtesans of the past would ensure that they had a tray of delicious delicacies to tempt and feed their lovers. A bite to eat between sex sessions can be just the thing to boost your energy levels once more, and it can even be a sexy event in itself, particularly if you choose finger foods which you can feed to one another.

Serve your boudoir banquet at a small table in the bedroom or on a beautiful breakfast tray. Imagine you are in a five star luxury hotel, and that you have just ordered room service; how would they do it? Make sure that you have napkins available so that sticky finger marks are not left on the bed linen, and if possible use red as your colour theme for crockery and glassware to make the event more romantic. Pink would work just as well. Heart-shaped plates are lovely to serve nibbles on and as the popular love heart actually derives from an old Norse rune which symbolized sex, this would be very appropriate for a boudoir feast. Light a few extra candles so that you can see what you are eating, and also because men like to watch women eat. Bearing this in mind, do try to consume your food in an alluring manner – take your inspiration from the sexy Cadbury Flake ads of the 1980s and 1990s! Take notice of how a man eats too as this could give away vital clues as to his love-making habits. If he rushes his food, taking the pleasure as quickly as possible, then he may well try to rush the sex act too, so that his hunger is satisfied quickly. On the other hand if he likes to savour his food, taking time to enjoy every bite, then he is more likely to savour every moment of love making and enjoy every last morsel you have to offer him. And if you are between boyfriends, then set up a table for one and book a private boudoir screening of Errol Flynn's finest moments – it could be one of the best dates you've had so far!

## Aphrodisiacs

Here are a few aphrodisiacs you might like to include in your boudoir banquet, by way of suggestion. Remember to include some carbohydrates to boost energy levels, so a selection of crackers and cheese served with a bunch of grapes would be a simple yet elegant feast if this is all you have available at short notice. Just remember to keep the snack light or you might never get to the encore performance!

*Chocolate*. The best known and most widely available aphrodisiac is of course chocolate, which releases those feel-good hormones associated with orgasm. This could be the reason why single women may tend to consume more chocolate. In the boudoir, use a chocolate fountain and dip in strawberries, marshmallow and chunks of fudge. Or keep a heart-shaped box filled with luxury chocolates from your favourite chocolatier. Alternatively indulge in a chocolate mousse, or chocolate body paint served up on your lover.

*Honey*. Honey is sacred to the love goddesses Aphrodite and Venus. It is sometimes referred to as the dew of love, and this could be why some men refer to female genitalia as the golden honey-pot! Honey is a staple ingredient of love spells and romantic dinner recipes. Its golden stickiness can make it a messy food, so try honey cakes, which are more manageable, or drink mead, which is made from honey and is said to keep men aroused and virile.

*Vanilla.* Sacred to Venus and also to Diana the moon goddess, vanilla is often used in romantic meals as an enticing flavour. Its warmth draws you in and it has aphrodisiac properties, so if all you have available is a tub of vanilla ice cream and two spoons then you are ready to go!

*Apple.* The forbidden fruit. Sharing an apple with a lover is said to ensure that your relationship flourishes and has longevity, so slice up a few Granny Smiths and feed them to one another.

*Banana.* Apart from the obvious phallic associations bananas are high in zinc, which can help to increase arousal and promote a strong libido – a great grown-up excuse for that old childhood favourite, banana custard.

*Asparagus.* This is another well-known aphrodisiac, which is said to inflame the lust of both men and women. Make sure it is dripping in butter and eat it provocatively!

*Tomatoes.* Tomatoes were once known as love apples because of their aphrodisiac qualities. They are widely available and can be used in many dishes.

*Strawberries.* Some fruits, such as the strawberry, resemble female genitalia when cut in half. Cut a strawberry, fig or avocado in half from top to bottom to reveal their alluring, erotic shape. This can help to make your man think instantly of sex, so add strawberries to your boudoir feast. Even better, dip them in dark chocolate and have them with champagne.

*Oysters.* Eating oysters is said to inflame and arouse passion. They can also increase stamina, which is why Kylie Minogue eats them mid-concert when she is on tour – perhaps that is the secret of her sex appeal and the reason behind the twinkle in her eyes! If you are planning an Olympic sex marathon then stock up on these sea food delicacies.

### Blessing of the Boudoir Feast

Once you have prepared your boudoir banquet and have laid it ready on a table or a tray, hold your hands over it, palms down and say the following words of blessing:

> *Great Goddess of love, bless this feast and infuse it with your gifts of passion and lust, that it might inflame our desire, rekindle our romance and inspire both of us to indulge in all the acts of pleasure which we so enjoy. Blessed be!*

Now light your boudoir candles and prepare to enjoy a night of magically fuelled passion and romance.

## Bad Bedroom Karma

Our environment can have a negative effect on our lives and how we feel. Areas and buildings can soak up energy like sponges, which is fine when people are happy and joyful, but not so good if any kind of negative event has occurred. Many people tend to feel nervous and jumpy when they are in a hospital, even if they are only visiting someone else, or if the event is a happy one, say for example the birth of a child. The illness confined within any hospital can cause negative energies to permeate the building and visitors often pick up on this at a subconscious level. Negative energies can be found anywhere and they do tend to create problems, making people feel lethargic and depressed, and even blocking positivity.

Your home is no different from any other building and it too can hold on to bad vibes left over from illness, bereavement or family squabbles. This of course extends into the boudoir, particularly if you have recently broken up with someone, had a row with your partner or suffered some other kind of relationship trauma. The negative energies can linger. The most common side effect of this is that your libido may become very low, and you might even start to feel quite depressed. Worse still, you might be surrounded by the bad vibes of awfully bad sex or the negative energies of an ex-boyfriend. Such a negative atmosphere might even block a new love from coming into your life and it can have a debilitating effect on your sexual relations in general. Fortunately a quick Wiccan cleansing ritual can clear away all those negative vibes, allowing more positive, earth-moving energies to take up residence instead.

## *Ritual to Banish Bad Boudoir Karma*

Ideally a witch would cleanse her entire home every month at the time of the new moon, but in the case of the boudoir more specific attention is needed and it is essential that you perform a cleansing ritual following a relationship break-up, an illness or an argument with your partner, in order to banish any lingering negativity.

First open the windows and allow fresh air to circulate. Then make a cleansing blend by adding two teaspoons of lemon juice and four drops of pine essential oil to 100ml of pure spring water. Keep this blend in a spritzer bottle and shake it well before going around your boudoir (or the whole house of you like) and spraying it with abandon. As you do so chant:

*Negative vibes which may linger here*
*I banish them all, this space is clear!*
*Sorrow and sadness, all are gone*
*Positivity reigns; this spell is done!*

Now play some loud music to energize the room, then redress the balance by switching to something more soothing and lighting a scented candle. Burning a stick of pine incense every week can also help to keep your space free of negative energy.

CHAPTER 6

# Flirt to Win!

All successful relationships are based on a foundation of positive and respectful communication. Yet much of our communication is actually non-verbal, so understanding the art of body language is essential if you want to play a good game of seduction. In addition to non-verbal communication men and women tend to banter playfully with one another, teasing and taunting their way into one another's affections, or perhaps even joking each other out of an ill humour. When both verbal and non-verbal communications are working together in a woman she can become a seriously provocative vamp and a powerful temptress. Great flirtation skills are essential in any *femme fatale*, and when they are used correctly they can set you apart from all the competition, giving you the seductive edge. But before we delve into the fascinating world of flirtation there are a few points to bear in mind:

- Flirtation should enhance your self-respect not diminish it in any way.
- It should be subtle rather than overt.
- It should be natural rather than contrived.
- It should not compromise your independence or your personal safety in any way.
- It should boost your self-esteem and confidence.

- It should entice and fascinate your target, not frighten him away.
- It should be elegant, dignified and sophisticated, not brazen or tarty.
- It should demonstrate your wit and intelligence, not make you look like a bimbo.
- It should be alluring rather than vulgar.
- The more flesh you have on display the less effective your flirtations will be.

## Feeling Flirty?

Everyone flirts to some degree whether they are aware of it or not. After all, flirtation is just another form of communication and a way of interacting with others. It need not have sexual connotations, for at its most basic it is simply about being polite, friendly and charming and exercising good manners. This is why flirtation skills are useful in any situation, not just the romantic kind. A good flirt will strike up a rapport with anyone, from either sex and of any age – even animals respond to a good flirt! The trick is to keep the flirtation to an appropriate level.

Try to think of flirtation as your personal love-light; a smouldering flame which burns within you and can never be extinguished. It is always there, so you might as well use it to your advantage. You are in control of this flame and of how brightly it burns. So in the bedroom feel free to stoke the fires up and get the heat going enough to work up a sweat! In the boardroom, however, or when chatting with friends, turn the love-light down to a steady simmer, emitting just enough warmth to make you appear friendly and approachable but not so much as to be inappropriate. In this way you can maintain a degree of control over the situation in which you find yourself. Flirting too outrageously with the boss could get you fired. Even worse, it could get you a promotion with strings attached.

I believe that everyone has the right to a little innocent flirtation, though I accept that some people do take this liberty too far and do not seem to know where to draw the line. Even married couples are entitled to a brief flirtation, providing it is innocent and not the precursor of an affair. There is nothing more flattering to the ego than having someone flirt with you, particularly when both parties are secure in the knowledge that the interaction is just harmless fun. To see a great example of innocent flirtation watch a couple of TV presenters at work and pay attention to the banter and innuendo which swings back and forth.

If you are out with your partner and you witness a little flirtation going on try not to get too upset. We all like to be flattered and it can be a great boost to the ego when a stranger finds you attractive, so try to be gracious enough to allow your man to enjoy the attention for a short time. When he catches your eye, as he surely will as soon as his guilt-trip kicks in, give him your sexiest smile and raise a quizzical brow to send him the message 'Hi, remember me? The hot-stuff you're going home with?' This always works (unless you are with a total love-rat!) and it will urge him to make a bit of a fuss of you for the rest of the evening. You can then enjoy a very smug moment when Flirty Miss has to watch you go home with your man for a night of unrestrained passion.

If the situation is reversed and someone is flirting with you then by all means be friendly and charming in return. Enjoy the attention for a few minutes then slip your arm through your man's in a show of solidarity before taking polite leave of your admirer. Of course it goes without saying that you should never go out of your way to make someone feel uncomfortable or insecure, so never flirt in revenge.

## Social Butterfly

The social butterfly is charming, sophisticated, well mannered, intelligent, good humoured, stylish and immaculately groomed. She is also a fantastic flirt and can have a room full of people eating out of her hand in a very short time. She is admired, imitated and generally well liked; if ever she is left out of someone's party list then it is either a terrible oversight or due to the fact that her presence is deemed to be too much of a threat.

Any woman can become a social butterfly, and this will greatly enhance her temptress style. It does not depend on money, wealth, status or fame. It is simply flirtation at its most sophisticated. Nor do you need a wide circle of friends. Everyone has a social circle, which generally includes family, friends and colleagues from work. Your social circle might also include people from various clubs and societies to which you belong. If you have children then the other mothers that you know are a part of your social circle.

How large or small your social circle is not really relevant, though the more groups of people you know the more events you are likely to be invited to. It could even be the case that you have a different image for different groups of people within your circle. For example you would not normally wear the same outfit to pick the children up from school as you would to attend a Wicca gathering as the two events require a completely different dress code. Your image will have a bearing on how you interact with people, whether you are aware of this or not.

Any social gathering is an opportunity for you to practise your flirtation skills. Start off the event with a low, simmering love-light and allow people to gravitate towards your warmth. Then as the night wears on turn it up a notch by singling out your target and perhaps chatting with him in a quiet corner somewhere, away from the crowd. Do not be too hot to handle though, as this could send him running for the hills. Men can feel threatened or cheated if a woman is too aggressive in her attentions, for such behaviour goes against the laws of nature, which state that as a rule men chase, women choose. The Wiccan temptress works *with* Mother Nature, not *against* her; so flirt by all means, but try not to actively pursue – that is his job and he will not thank you for robbing him of it!

Whatever situation you find yourself in do try to think of yourself as a social butterfly, whether at the office party, a family wedding or a night out with the girls. Even if you are simply out enjoying some retail therapy, try to think of yourself as the sexy goddess of the malls! Wherever you go, whatever you do, you are a social butterfly: looking good, feeling great, radiating sensual warmth and sex appeal as you go about your busy day.

Remember too that every event you attend has the potential to become a romantic rendezvous – even if that just means kick-starting your long-term lover into demonstrating some love. If you are single and content to remain so then every event is the opportunity to turn a few heads and be noticed for all the right reasons. The most successful *femme fatale* can get anyone to like her, whether a man, a woman, a child or a four-legged friend. She can win anyone over by being approachable, kind and respectful, and by turning on the charm.

Effective flirtation is not a narcissistic act, but a powerful social tool. It is not necessarily about drawing attention to yourself, but more about making other people feel good about themselves, and enjoying positive interactions with those around you. Bearing all of this in mind here are a few tips for improving your flirtation skills and for turning yourself into an elegant social butterfly.

- Smile! When you smile you will look friendly, approachable and far more glamorous.
- Walk tall and with purpose. Even if you are only walking to your car, keep your head up and look ahead to where you are going.
- Make eye contact with people when you are in conversation with them. Nothing is more rude than staring around the room when someone it talking to you.
- Listen. A good flirt knows how to talk; a great flirt knows how to listen. We have two ears and only one mouth so we should all be listening twice as much as we talk. Verbal incontinence is not sexy.
- Take your cue from those around you, especially when it comes to greetings and farewells. Just remain relaxed and still and let

the other person decide if it's going to be a handshake, a kiss or a warm hug. Not everyone has a tactile nature, so in taking a passive approach you place them in control of how close they want to get. This will save you from embarrassing moments.

- Talk their language. Pick up on the words and phrases they use and repeat them in your conversation to build a rapport. If you are trying to get to know someone from another country, learn to say a few words in their language to help them feel more at ease; pick simple words such as hello, thank you and goodbye.
- Make an entrance. When walking into a room pause for a moment in the open door to let everyone see you have arrived. The draught from the door will make people look your way, so make sure you are looking fabulous and are wearing your best smile. Enjoy the attention for a second and then move into the room and mingle.
- Make an elegant exit. When leaving, again pause in the doorway; then turn slightly and look back over your shoulder at someone you have been chatting with that evening. Catch his eye, smile and give him a sexy wave before gliding out of the door. This is guaranteed to make him wish he had got your phone number – he might even come running after you!
- Never invade someone's personal space unless you are invited to do so. This rule applies everywhere from the dance floor to the queue at the bank. It is very bad manners to breathe down a stranger's neck.
- Above all else, maintain your dignity at all times and in any event. Whatever the circumstances may be, conduct yourself with decorum and propriety.

Once you have mastered these simple techniques enhance your social skills with a little Wiccan magic by performing the following spell.

### Transcendence Spell

As a magical symbol the butterfly represents transcendence and the natural transformation of one thing into another. Just as the lowly caterpillar becomes a beautiful butterfly, so you can become a beautiful social butterfly and a popular member of your social circle.

First take two sheets of paper and cut out two large butterfly shapes. On these shapes write down identical lists of all the social graces you would like to have or develop. If you are shy, for example, then write down the word 'confidence'; if you know that you have a tendency towards outrageous behaviour then write the words 'dignity' and 'decorum'. Whatever you feel you may lack on a personal level, write it down on your lists. Now say:

> *Venus and Aphrodite, gracious goddesses of love and beauty, assist me in my quest to be full of social graces. Help me to take control of my destiny; to mould my character; and to manifest the charms and attributes of a social butterfly. This is my spell of transcendence. So mote it be!*

Now take your two identical butterfly lists and place one copy on your dressing table where you will see it every day. Burn the other list in a heatproof bowl to release the magic, giving thanks to the goddesses of love and beauty as you do so.

## Read My Body Language

I have already said that many of our flirtations and communications are actually non-verbal, and our body certainly does have a language all of its own. What is more, the body cannot keep a secret, so if you are attracted to or annoyed with someone, your body language will give you away.

Reading and using body language is a core skill of any good

temptress, and learning to read it well can help you to get beyond the lip service which someone might be paying you and extract the hidden truth of any situation, which can be a useful trick to have up your sleeve. First, however, you must learn to be more aware of your own body language so that you can gain control over the subtle signs you are sending out into the world. Here are some of the key ways to become the most attractive and desirable woman in the room, and of course to let someone know that you are interested.

- Smile confidently, chat, but listen closely too. Maintain eye contact.
- Keep your body open and approachable so do not sit with arms and legs crossed, or shield yourself by holding tightly on to a drink, a book or your handbag. Stay open and relaxed. Face into the room and look friendly.
- When chatting with someone you really like lean into the conversation slightly. Look at his lips as he talks then regain eye contact as you flick your hair back seductively, giving him a glimpse of your neck.
- Turn your whole body towards him in order to engage fully with him, rather as though you were his mirror image. When two people are tuned into one another they will synchronize their movements; picking up their drinks at the same time, standing in the same way etc. Tune into him by mirroring his stance and movements.
- Block out the rest of the room, either by altering your position or by using props, such as a menu. Develop a feeling of intimacy and being alone together, ignoring the background noise and concentrating only on your partner. Make him believe that he is the only man in the room.

By contrast the body also has subtle ways of telling someone to stay back, go away, do not come any closer. Here are some classic body language techniques guaranteed to freeze someone out.

- Avoid all eye contact at all times and do not smile.
- Keep your body language closed, so fold your arms and cross your legs. Turn away from the person who is invading your space.
- Use the objects around you as a shield; nurse your handbag, hold your glass in front of your chest, pretend to be engrossed in a book or the menu.
- If you have long hair, allow it to fall forward and hide behind it.
- If all else fails and he is still persistent, tell him clearly to go away. Be firm and frosty, but do spare a thought for his feelings as no one likes to be rejected. There is no need to descend into bitchiness.
- Always try your best not to send out mixed signals. Be clear about what you want your body to say and to whom; it is going to speak on your behalf anyway, so you might as well give it a script!

## What Is He Saying?

Learning to take charge of and use your own body language is really only half the story. Now you need to understand what his body language is saying. Picking up on the subtle signs which you might otherwise miss is a good way to increase your powers as a temptress.

*Signs he is interested.* If he is attracted to you he will raise his eyebrows slightly each time you first make eye contact. This is usually followed by a smile and an attempt to come close enough to speak to you, without making an obvious bee-line.

Encourage him with open body language and a friendly face. He will also watch you as you move around the room, so stay sexy!

*Signs he is thinking about having sex with you.* If he is mesmerized by your lips as you speak he is probably thinking about kissing you. When he is gearing up to make his move he is likely to lean towards you, perhaps supporting himself on the wall behind you – this blocks out any other man who is thinking of trying his luck and warns off any competition. He might also try to draw attention to his hips by hooking his thumb in his jeans pocket, or thrusting slightly forwards – he wants you to be aware of his family jewels! Encourage him with a flick of the hair and by placing your hand at your throat so that you can trace your neck and collar bone with your finger.

*Signs he likes you but he is shy.* If he is catching your eye, smiling at you and hovering nearby without actually making a move, then he could be struggling with shyness. Wait a while for him to pluck up courage, and if he still has not spoken to you make it easier by asking him a simple non-sexual question. This gives him the opportunity to strike up a conversation with you so give him all the encouragement he needs.

*Signs of deceit.* Lies are a form of fiction so if someone is telling fibs their eyes usually flick to the right, engaging the creative side of their brain. Touching the nose is another give-away that some sort of deception is going on. Being aware of these very subtle signs can help you to determine when your man is lying to you.

## Flirtation Spell

Now that you have all the skills of flirtation at your disposal you are ready to put them to the test on your next big night out. But before you leave the house enhance your chances of success by performing this simple spell.

As you get ready, light a tea-light and focus on the flame. Imagine yourself flirting and being the object of every man's attention. Then repeat this incantation three times:

*Sexy, sultry, feeling flirty*
*Getting dressed to kill.*
*Hips are swaying, undulating*
*Seeking love's sweet thrill.*
*Chatting, laughing, smile flashing*
*Catching every gaze.*
*From crimson lips seduction drips*
*Enjoying wanton ways!*

Allow the tea-light to burn for as long as you are preparing for your night out, then blow out the flame.

## The Magic of Make-up

The real flirtation actually begins when you prepare for an event – when you are grooming yourself into provocative perfection, styling your hair, choosing your ensemble, applying make-up and seducing yourself along the way! This is when you begin to imagine yourself having a wonderful time, meeting nice people and generally having lots of fun. You might even flirt with yourself in the mirror to a certain degree!

Wearing cosmetics is one of the joys of a woman's life. Most of us found our mother's make-up case when we were little girls and took delight in it, experimenting with complete abandon. I know I was always fascinated watching my mother getting ready to go out, and would sit on her bed watching closely as she applied powders, shadows and gloss. I can still recall the scent of her favourite perfume, and even now this it takes me back to my girlhood.

Cosmetics are the tools of the flirt and they should be regarded as every woman's friend. With just a few strokes of a make-up brush, you can give yourself a new image, hide an imperfection or draw attention to your best features. You can look dramatic, sultry, vibrant, cool, demure or innocently girly, simply by choosing certain shades and applying them in a particular way. You can look naturally flawless by making use of tinted moisturizers and lip balms; or you can create a signature look for yourself which then becomes your trademark.

The practice of wearing cosmetics is far from new; people have been painting their faces for centuries. From early people applying their war paint (still a slang term for make-up) to Queen Elizabeth I wearing her lead-based face powder, to the modern cosmetics industry worth billions of pounds, make-up has been a part of every era. Some items have even achieved cult status: red lipstick, for example, is the trademark of any siren. A woman's mouth is thought to remind men of vaginal lips. So painting the lips red facilitates this imagery – small wonder that red lipstick is the trademark of many iconic women and sex symbols over the years, from Marilyn Monroe to Dita von Teese.

In certain cultures make-up also had a magical purpose and each type of cosmetic had a ritualistic basis. Woad, for example, was painted on warriors to make them look more intimidating and so undermine the confidence of their opponents. In Egypt the eyes were heavily made up for two reasons: first to ward off the evil eye and all its negative effects, and secondly to honour the god Horus, whose symbol is the eye of protection.

The practice of painting the lips also has magical connotations. Aside from the seductiveness of painting them red, in the past people believed that lip paint could help to protect them from being poisoned. It was also thought to prevent possession by evil spirits. Nowadays red lips have very different associations. By wearing red lipstick a woman is drawing attention to her sexuality and her attractiveness. Any Wiccan temptress worth her wand would be lost without her favourite red lipstick! So the next time you are applying your make-up, remember that you are continuing an ancient tradition which is steeped in magic and folklore.

Use your cosmetics with reverence and with a magical purpose in mind. Try these handy tips:

- Wear black eye liner to protect yourself in general and to give yourself a sultry, smoky look. The more eye liner you wear the more dramatic your eyes will become, giving you a feline look which is very sexy.
- Wearing green eye liner and eye shadow could help to ward away jealousy, particularly if it is coming from other women, and known rivals.
- Wear a strong red lipstick if you want to get intimate with a lover, or you want to attract someone new as it will turn you into a complete vamp.
- Wear a bright red lipstick if you need to confront someone about something and you want them to take notice of what you have to say. Likewise if you need to give a speech of some sort.
- Wear pale pinks and peaches if you are feeling vulnerable and fragile and want to invoke your lover's protective instincts.
- Wear icy blues and silver if you need to freeze someone out.

*Draw attention to your best bits using jewellery. Your favourite body part need not be sexual; Angelina Jolie allegedly claims that her hands are her favourite feature. I love my wrists and wear three-quarter sleeves and a bracelet to show them off. Take a good look at yourself and find out what you like best about your body, then draw attention to that part of yourself. If you have slender ankles wear an ankle chain; if you have pretty feet have a professional pedicure; if you love your shoulders wear halter neck tops and a gorgeous shimmering body powder.*

## Siren Secret

*True flirtation is not about baring all to the world or indulging in outrageous behaviour. It is far more intelligent and sophisticated than that, and it works on sound psychological principles. Keep in mind that you can flirt with anyone, providing your love-light is at the correct level for the situation. Practise flirting as you go about your daily life. Note what works for you and what you find to be particularly effective. Start to think of yourself as a great flirt, someone who can enjoy positive interactions with anyone else and in any situation.*

CHAPTER 7

# Aiming Cupid's Arrow

You will have very little chance of achieving your dreams if you do not know exactly what it is you want. To be successful in any field you must first of all set yourself a goal and then keep it in sight. If you are not completely sure what you want from a romantic relationship then how can you expect to be fulfilled and happy with your lover? By the same token, if you are not clear about what kind of attributes your Mr Right should have, how can you expect to find him, or recognize him when he crosses your path?

If you are already in an established relationship then you should still be setting goals, as they will help to keep your relationship interesting and exciting. Monotony is the bane of many long-term relationships and might even be their undoing. This is because people quite naturally become bored when they are faced with the same thing day in and day out. We need our intelligence to be stretched and stimulated in order to remain interested in something – and this includes romance! Keeping the wow factor in a relationship requires commitment and imagination on both sides, so setting goals which you can work towards together can help to keep the fizz in the relationship. You will also have the thrill of a joint goal accomplished. It need not be a huge undertaking: it could be as simple as putting aside money for the romantic holiday of a lifetime. But whatever the target you choose to set, its accomplishment will become a milestone in your relationship, and something which you can look back on as a couple. The longer you have been together the more important it is that you keep sharing new experiences, that you work towards maintaining the excitement and that you try to make your time together as interesting as possible.

## The Ethics of Love Magic

Love is universal. To deprive someone of love can cause no end of mental and emotional problems. It is vital to our well-being – indeed to our very existence. It gives us strength and courage to face adversity; it bucks us up when we are feeling down; it guides us forward when we lose our way; it can double our joys and triumphs, ease our burdens and halve our troubles. Love makes us feel we can do anything, achieve any goal, realize any dream.

When you give yourself in love to someone else you are entrusting them with the greatest of all treasures. Your emotional well-being and peace of mind depends on the love you have given being nurtured, protected, respected and cared for. Some people will have had the misfortune of giving their love to someone who was not worthy to receive it, who treated them badly and left them broken hearted. Perhaps we all need to go through such an experience in order to recognize the real thing when it comes along.

Love itself does not have a dark side, for it is all purity and goodness. But when love is taken for granted, disrespected, betrayed or rejected, we are left picking up the pieces of our lives and trying to put them back together again. This type of experience can lead us to close ourselves off from love, to distrust it and even to reject it outright. Yet it was not love that let us down – only the recipient did that. It is a hard lesson to learn, but the fact that so many people choose to take the risk again with someone new is proof that love is definitely worth it, and being open to it is vital to us if we wish to thrive. Like a flower without sunlight, a life without love is no life at all.

There are no spells which can make someone love you; love

cannot be forced. It is a gift that is given freely, spirit to spirit, heart to heart, in perfect love and perfect trust. However the basic seed of attraction can be nurtured until it blossoms into love and a relationship begins, and magic can help such seeds to bloom. As with all kinds of magic though, there are certain rules which must be abided by when casting any kind of love spell.

## *The Importance of Free Will*

Witches believe in free will – everyone has the right to make their own choices in life. When free will is compromised rebellion begins. Nobody likes to feel that they have no control over their own lives, that their destiny is being determined by another. Nobody likes to feel like a puppet whose lover is pulling the strings. However, some personalities are so strong that a weaker person may find themselves constantly giving way and the relationship becomes unbalanced, with all the power on one side rather than being evenly distributed.

Freedom of choice is every person's right, and when someone takes away this choice they are committing the worst kind of disrespect. It goes without saying that if you love someone you should respect them and honour their free will by allowing them to make their own choices and decisions, even if they choose the very opposite of what you want.

All magic should be cast with a regard for free will, so think very carefully before casting any kind of spell. If you have the slightest suspicion that it could work against a person's free will, then do not cast it but find an alternative or a non-magical solution to the situation. Contrary to popular belief, witches do not go around casting spells on people, or hexing handsome strangers into bed! Such types of magic are in complete opposition to the most basic of Wiccan rules, the Wiccan Rede which states, 'An it harm none, do what you will'. Bending someone's will to your own desires is a form of magical harm, and using any kind of spell to make another person do what you want is against the rules. True witches just do not do that sort of thing.

Does this mean that witches are powerless, or that they cannot use magic to improve their lot romantically? Far from it. But rather than trying to impose our wishes on another person, we cast spells around ourselves, our homes and our environments in order to influence events in a positive way. In this way we can positively enhance our communication and interaction with others without impinging on their free will and without breaking the 'harm none' code of Wiccan ethics.

By the same token witches do not cast spells to gain the affections of a specific individual, as not only would this compromise the subject's free will, it might even bring about a disastrous relationship instead of the love's young dream you were hoping for. This is because you cannot always trust your lust to lead you in the most appropriate direction, and a negative relationship following a spell of magic would be just the thing to undermine your confidence in your abilities. The person you admire might not be right for you for any number of reasons. You just do not know from a pleasant chat in a bar or a smile across the water cooler.

So if you cannot bewitch a sex-god into your bed, lure away your rival's husband or cast a spell on the boy next door, what can you do? You can work magic to draw love into your life in all its many incarnations, or to summon a new lover as yet unknown to you, or to enhance existing partnerships, or even to surround yourself with the healing essence of love when you are recovering from a romantic disaster. All such forms of magic are permissible. And rest assured that if the man you have a crush on is the one for you, then this spell craft will draw him like a bee to honey. And if he is not the one, the universe will send someone much better who *is* right for you. So you see, you really have nothing to lose if you play by the Wiccan rules, and everything to gain.

## Make Yourself Lovable

The Wiccan temptress knows that there is no shortage of love in the world, only people who misuse it. Love is all around us every day and it comes in many guises, from parental and family love to the bond you share with your friends, the passion you feel for a lover, or the unconditional love you share with your pets. There should be no reason for anyone to feel unloved. Some people might feel a little lonely from time to time, but I believe that loneliness is nature's way of making us appreciate relationships more. And prolonged loneliness is really a lifestyle choice, not a disability. It might sound harsh but if you have been lonely for a long period of time then it is largely your own fault, as the world is full of people just waiting to be met – but you have to put the effort in.

The Wiccan temptress knows those traits which make a person lovable and exudes them in her personality. She knows that confidence, dignity, intellect, self-respect, respect for others, tolerance and a sense of humour are what make someone attractive. She knows that patience, compassion, empathy, kindness and a gentle nature are what make a person lovable. Furthermore it is not the desire to *be* loved which makes someone lovable, but rather the desire *to* love and to try to love unconditionally. This is no easy task, as we all go into a relationship with certain expectations and if your partner does not quite measure up then it can be all too tempting to withhold affection and use love as a weapon. But this will not make you lovable.

To become more lovable pay more attention to how you interact with others. Are you polite, respectful and tolerant? Are you confident and independent? Do you show empathy, compassion and patience in your dealings with people? Try to bring all these qualities to every interaction you have in order to make yourself more lovable, approachable and pleasant to be with. If you are not fun to be around, why would anyone want to spend time getting to know you? Be charming, flirty and sweet natured, but most of all be lovable.

## The Art of Fascination

The word fascinate comes from the Latin *fascinare* which means 'to bewitch'. I think it is a lovely word and if a man tells me that I am fascinating or captivating I take it as the highest compliment. It is much more complimentary than being told I am beautiful, as whatever small measure of beauty I might have will fade with time, while my ability to fascinate should improve over the years as I gain in maturity and life experience. This kind of compliment also indicates that the man in question has acknowledged my inner goddess and has witnessed my 'witchyness' and that he is suitably charmed by both. This is exactly the way it should be!

A woman's ability to fascinate men and women alike does not depend on her looks, so whatever gifts nature did or did not bestow upon you, you can still fascinate and captivate with the best of them. Captivation literally means to hold someone captive, to ensnare them with your charm and wit so that they are perfectly content to spend as much time with you as possible. This goes for female as well as male friends. You should aim to captivate and fascinate everyone you meet, as it is the very best way to make new friends and to expand your social circle.

So how do you go about fascinating someone? Fascination could be said to be the basic magic of good manners, good conversation and a great sense of humour. These are the basic requirements. To this you must add all the skills of a lovable, popular social butterfly and, even more important, you should aim to set yourself apart from the group in some way so that people instantly feel that they have never met anyone quite like you – which they have not for you are unique.

By drawing attention to your individuality in a modest way you are weaving a web in which to captivate your audience. Once you have grabbed their attention with your sophisticated charm, fascinate them by allowing a touch of your quirkiness to shine through and by revealing to them a more hidden facet of your personality, such as your interest in goddess power, or the fact that you are reading this book. Tell them of your passions. The key is to draw them into your world slightly by showing how approachable and grounded you are, how sophisticated and alluring, and then wow them by throwing an unusual fact into the mix, thus setting yourself apart from the crowd. Then let the fascination begin! Once you reach this stage of the game, chat for five or ten minutes and then move on, leaving your target dying to know more. As you circulate the room he will undoubtedly find a way to bump into you again, and you will know your temptress trick has worked when he says something like, 'So tell me more about ...' This is the art of fascination and it works like the charm it is. Bear in mind that the hidden detail you reveal about yourself should be personal but not private, so *do not* tell him about your fondness for thigh high boots and a riding crop, but *do* tell him that you moonlight as a poet and are giving a recital of your work at a local wine bar at the weekend. Fascination depends on your coming across as interesting and intriguing, not freaky or geeky!

## The Love Goddess Altar

Setting up a love altar is a great way to aim Cupid's arrow and draw more love into your life. An altar will act as a magical magnet, drawing romance, passion and love towards you on a daily basis. It will also help to enhance the energies of an established relationship, bringing magic to your bond of love and strengthening the partnership you have.

Setting aside a space in your home and dedicating it to love is a positive step towards becoming a powerful temptress. Many men are intrigued by the idea of witches and witchcraft to some degree, and they will be fascinated to see a love altar tucked away in a corner of the boudoir. Do bear in mind, however, that love has many faces and your altar should reflect all of these rather than romantic love alone.

To begin with decide where you want your love altar to be. I would recommend setting it up in the boudoir, preferably in a place where you can see it from your bed. Use any surface you have available, so a mantelpiece, a small table, a shelf or a chest of drawers would all be ideal. If you want to lay a pink or red scarf over it this will create a sense of romance and warmth, and will protect your furniture from candle drippings. Now create the altar as you want, ensuring that you include something from each of the categories below to make it reflect all aspects of love.

*Divine love.* In the centre of the altar you should place a representation of divine love, so a statue of a love goddess such as Aphrodite or Venus would be ideal. Alternatively use a representation of Diana, Gaia, an angel, a mermaid or an elemental. Sea shells represent the divine feminine too, so if all you have available is a large shell, this could create the centre piece of a natural and abstract altar.

*Family and pets.* Love from family and a pet is the very first love we are exposed to so on the left side of the altar place an item which represents this, such as a photograph. Add a rose quartz or amethyst crystal to keep this area of your life strong and healthy.

*Romantic love.* On the right-hand side of the altar place a photograph of you and your partner sharing a happy time together – a wedding picture is perfect. If you are single place a representation of a loving couple here, such as a fine art card or a statue. Add a carnelian crystal to this area, to keep the warmth of love in your life and relationship.

*Passion.* Add lots of candles to represent burning passion and to illuminate your life with love's light. Add a mermaid picture or statue to reflect your own siren energies.

*Incense.* Keep an incense burner somewhere on the altar so that you can safely burn your chosen incenses on a daily basis. This is an ancient way of connecting with divinity and sending your wishes out into the universe, and it will help to keep the altar free of negative energies.

*Optional additions.* If you wish you can add flowers, further crystals, heart-shaped trinket boxes, love spoons, romantic tokens, wedding album etc., to make your altar even more personal to you and your temptress dreams.

Once your altar is set up light the candles and burn your chosen incenses to dedicate the space to love and romance. Spend time at your altar as often as you can. Ideally you should spend a few moments here communing with the Goddess before you retire to bed each night. Contemplate love in all its forms and give thanks for the way it enriches your life. The more time you spend at your love goddess altar the more in tune with love's vibrations you will become and the easier it will be to magnetize love and passion into your life and your relationships.

Make sure you keep your altar clean and tidy, but do not be afraid to make changes to it. An altar will change over time, as its purpose is to reflect who you are now and who you would like to become in the future, rather than who you were six months or a year ago. Change it to suit your lifestyle and circumstances. Enjoy this space, for it is the heart of all your romantic hopes and dreams.

## Making Your Mind Up

There will probably come a time when you will need to sit down and take stock of your life so far, deciding what it is you want from a relationship and also what you are prepared to give. Too many people go blindly into a romantic liaison, without discussing such vital things as values, faith, core beliefs, whether or not they want children and so on. This can very easily lead to disaster, down the line.

A relationship is like a ship with two captains at the helm. Both must decide on a course for their voyage and then each take turns at the wheel to keep the ship on the agreed course. They should be equal, seeing their roles in terms of a job-share rather than as master and servant. If the captains cannot agree where to take the ship, or if they never even discuss their voyage together, then the ship will drift and eventually flounder. And the fault will lie not with the ship, but with its captains.

The very best time to decide what you want from a relationship and a partner is while you are still single. In this way you will give the universe clear instructions as to what you feel you need on a personal level and what you are not prepared to put up with. It is rather like placing a cosmic order for your dream man, rather than having to drift aimlessly through countless unsuitable suitors. If you are already in a relationship then deciding where you want it to go and how it should develop is something that should be discussed in the early stages of commitment.

To draw your ideal man into your life sit down with a sheet of paper and do some brainstorming. Write down all the things you want him to be, listing his physical attributes, his personal qualities and his general outlook on life. Be detailed in your descriptions. Does he have a positive attitude, is he good with finances, is he a sporty, outdoor type, must he adore horses? Make him as real in your mind as you can. Then on a second sheet of paper write down everything you are not prepared to put up with – the deal breakers. 'Married' should be top of this list! If you do not stipulate his single status you could meet your ideal man only to discover that he is already taken and off the market. Also on this list you might include such things as laziness, egotism, materialism, moodiness, greed, etc. Once you have both your lists roll them into a scroll and perform this spell.

## Angel of Love Summoning Spell

Go to your altar and take with you a red candle, a red ribbon and your scroll. Place the candle in a suitable holder and light it. Now call on the angel of love in the following way:

*Angel of love I call on you and summon you into my life;*
*Please bring your gifts of love and romance on the universal tide.*
*Fill my heart with glowing love, let passion's spirit reign.*
*I offer this spell from me to you, my ideal man to gain.*

Now read the scrolls out loud, then roll them up again and tie them with a red ribbon. Leave them in the romantic love section on the right hand side of your altar, then say:

*Angel of love, being of light*
*Epic romance is written in starlight.*
*Bring him to me, across land or sea*
*My true love I summon, so mote it be!*

Allow the candle to burn down naturally and wait for your true love to make himself known to you. This is a strong working of magic and you are asking for a big prize. It might therefore take up to a year to manifest, so be patient and have faith. The sooner you cast the spell, the sooner he will be in your life.

## True Love's First Kiss

The first kiss between two people is very important. We were brought up on fairy tales conditioning us to believe that a kiss bestowed with a true heart could work miracles, including waking up Sleeping Beauty and bringing Snow White back from the dead. So it is hardly surprising that when a man rubs lips with us we expect nothing less than fireworks, earthquakes, magic! While men might tend to think of kissing as a preliminary, to us it is one of the main events. And a great kiss really is magical. It sets your heart racing and your palms tingling and it makes you shiver from the inside out.

When I was seventeen a young man I had been fond of for some time finally plucked up the courage to kiss me – and his kiss blew me away. Perhaps this was because I had been so desperate for him to like me, or because he was six years older and seemed very mature and sophisticated to my teenage eyes. Whatever the reason, I saw stars that night – it was the kiss of a lifetime! And I will keep the treasured memory for ever, to relive whenever the mood takes me.

A first kiss needs to be just right. It needs to fit the girl just as well as Cinderella's shoe. It should be tender, a little cautious maybe, light and, above all, romantic. The man should be fully aware of the privilege you are bestowing on him – and vice versa of course. Give him the hint by looking directly at his lips, then tearing your eyes away as if your desire for him is all too much. A barely audible sigh works wonders too!

You can learn a great deal from that first kiss. If he gently cups your face with his hands and his kiss is feather light then he is likely to be a careful and considerate lover. If, on the other hand, he is devouring your face in what he obviously believes to be passion then he could well prove to be a greedy and selfish lover. Needless to say the first kiss should be an enchanting experience, and it should keep moisture to the minimum – if he has only just found out your name, he really has no business trying to get acquainted with your tonsils!

## First Kiss Spell

If you are hoping that tonight is the night for the kiss of a lifetime then repeat this incantation before and after you apply your lipstick.

*When his gaze meets mine*
*Let him not be remiss.*
*Leave us locked in a moment of time*
*Awaiting true love's first kiss.*
*Soft as a feather*
*The lightest touch*
*To remember for ever*
*This kiss means so much!*

## The Kiss of Eros

Eros is the Greek god of love, the equivalent to the Roman Cupid, but while Cupid has been reduced over time to the image of a chubby baby, Eros has maintained his standing as an athletic young man cavorting with pretty wood nymphs. The word 'erotic' comes from his name, and he certainly is erotic, sexy, lustful, yet as the son of Aphrodite he is also respectful of women and of the divine feminine. No one can put a zing in a kiss quite like Eros can, so call on him silently when your man leans in:

*Light as a feather, let Eros hover*
*Upon the sweet lips of my lover.*

### Temptress Tip

*To keep your lips kissably soft apply a little moisturizer to an old toothbrush and sprinkle this with fine sea salt. Pout and gently scrub the brush over your lips to exfoliate them. Rinse well and then apply your favourite tinted lip balm or your signature red pout.*

### Siren Secret

*Experiencing and enjoying romantic love is your Goddess-given right, so make full use of all the spells and hints in this chapter to find your dream man and set him in your sights as your target. Work some seduction magic which is free of negative consequences and harms none. Remember to play by the Wiccan rules and you will soon be enjoying love's sweet favours.*

CHAPTER 8

# *Reeling Him In*

You have grabbed your man's attention and begun a relationship. Now you need to keep his interest, and the best way to do that is to present yourself as a challenge he simple cannot help responding to. This is not about playing games or being manipulative, nor is it an anti-feminist approach. Far from it. It is simply working with Mother Nature and in accordance with her rules.

Men love a challenge; you only have to see them playing sports or working out the intricacies of self assembly furniture to see that. They also tend to be very competitive in their careers and they enjoy beating others to a promotion and climbing the corporate ladder. The compelling need to respond to a challenge is in their genes. Modern men still have the instincts of the hunter, which is probably just as strong as the feminine maternal instinct, and when it comes to the mating game we are not so far removed from our cave-dwelling ancestors as we would like to believe. This hunter instinct is largely the reason why men do the chasing and women do the choosing. He will not thank you for making the chase too easy for him, as you are effectively robbing him of a victory. When he does eventually catch up with you the relationship will be all the more precious to him. This concept is not an old-fashioned or outdated notion, and it is by no means anti-feminist – it is basic biology.

A clever temptress knows that by playing Mother Nature's game she is in fact empowering herself; she is giving herself the best possible chance of a happy, fulfilling relationship, one in which she is an equal partner and her independence is not compromised in any way. A smart witch always works with nature, not against her, and in presenting herself as a challenge she is playing up to a man's natural instincts.

This basically means that if you have just fallen in love, got married or had a baby, now is the time for you to do something just for yourself. Do something just for fun: sign up for a dance or yoga class, have a night out with the girls, take a weekend break with your mother and your sister, or your best friend. In this way your actions make a clear statement; you are carving out your role as an independent woman, despite the changes in your life circumstances. So what if you are a newly-wed, or a new mother? This should not mean that you become a mere shadow of the woman you were before. Marriage and motherhood should enhance the joy of a woman's life, not dissipate it. And if like me you are single and child free then you have no excuse *not* to be living a full and interesting life. You should make the very most of your freedom by indulging in hobbies and sports, travel, nights out, etc. It may be that you love the single life and have no desire to change your status, or that you will not be single for very much longer. Either way rather than staying at home get out and about and enjoy your liberty to the full.

## Absence Makes the Heart Grow Fonder

The fastest way to lose a man is to become Miss Needy overnight. Tuning yourself from the sexy person he was originally attracted to into a weak, clingy barnacle will do your love life no good at all, and if you regularly play this role then you are undermining your own confidence and compromising your independence and self-esteem.

You do not need a man in your life to be complete. Everything you need is already within you, and no one else can make you happy until you are happy within and by yourself. I believe that a loving partner will reflect your own internal happiness back at you, and will enhance the feelings of joy in your life. I do not believe that it is down to anyone else to make me happy. I am in charge of my own happiness and, while romance can enhance it, my personal happiness is not dependent on a romantic attachment. And if you are unhappy in yourself then no relationship will ever make you happy.

A relationship should be regarded as the icing on life's cake rather than the core ingredient for the cake itself. If you think of yourself as an independent individual, then you are the cake! And you will soon come to see that your life can be enjoyed with or without icing.

And spare a thought for your partner's independence too. Everyone needs breathing space and time to themselves. If your man is spending every night in the pub, working lots of overtime, or volunteering for every overseas trip available, then face up to the possibility that he could be trying to get away from you. He may need some time and space to himself for a while. Take the hint and encourage him to enjoy his independence; do not smother him. He is likely to be all the more considerate on his return, as he will have had time to appreciate you from a distance. This works both ways of course, and you should make the most of your own time if your partner is absent. Catch up with old friends, make new ones, resume an old hobby, join a gym. Consider taking up night classes to further your education. In short, get a life! Dependency is not cute, it is not sexy and it is certainly not temptress behaviour.

Absence really does make the heart grow fonder so allow your relationship space to breathe by taking time out and allowing yourself to miss one another. It is human nature to want what everyone else has and nothing is more desirable than popularity. Make yourself less available to the man of the moment and a little more available to friends and family. Never let a man think that he is the centre of your universe; do not cancel other arrangements in favour of spending more time with him and never allow your life to revolve around him.

In keeping busy and independent you will both appreciate the time that you do spend together more, and it will feel more special. Needless to say, when you *are* spending time together you should give one another your full and undivided attention. Maintaining your individuality and personal independence will enable him to see what a well-grounded, self-sufficient woman you are. As a result he will come to value your integrity and he will work hard to spend time with you, appreciating you as a unique individual and not just another girlfriend. What is more, because it will be clear that you do not actually need him, he is less likely to harbour the fear that you have a hidden agenda or a five-year plan to get hitched and hatched as soon as possible.

## Blessing of Feminine Independence

Artemis is the Greek goddess of feminine independence. She is a lunar virgin goddess and her energies can be invoked to help you develop and maintain your own independence. As a huntress she is associated with woodlands, forests and the natural landscape. She is a divine protector of all women and children and she is said to guard womankind from masculine violence. Her sacred animals are deer, stags and hounds. She is also closely linked with all felines and her association with the domestic cat led to her becoming known as the witch's goddess, especially during the witch hunts of the Middle Ages.

To invoke Artemis's blessing of independence in your life, light a tea-light and say the following incantation:

*Artemis of woodland ways*
*Enchant me with your lunar rays.*
*I give my spirit unto you*
*Please make me feisty, strong and true*
*Loving independently*
*Enjoying freedom's liberty.*
*In loving trust I call to thee*
*This is my will, so mote it be.*

Allow the tea-light to burn down naturally. Repeat the spell whenever you feel that your independence is being compromised and needs a bit of a boost.

## Motherhood

At some stage in your relationship you might start to get a little broody, and having a baby will be at the top of your list of priorities, particularly if you feel that time is running out. Personally I have yet to be convinced that the female body clock actually exists. If it does, then mine must be digital for I have never heard it ticking away my fertile years. Perhaps this is because when it comes to babies and motherhood I seem to be missing the 'Ahhhh!' gene. However, I am fully aware that many women want to join in the baby race. Many claim to have found their greatest happiness in motherhood, and having children is of course a natural part of a woman's life. It is also a step forward in a relationship if that is what you both want.

Becoming a mother is not a decision to be taken lightly and you should take into account all the implications of such a change to your life circumstances. Too many people buy into what I call the mythology of motherhood, believing it to be a blissful rendition of a baby-products advertisement, where parenting is naturally easy, and the baby is stench free and sleeps all the time!

Motherhood is an irreversible state and the only job in the world where you cannot hand in your notice when it all gets too much. And it is despicable to trick a man into parenthood by becoming 'accidentally' pregnant in order to gain a long-term relationship or marriage. Apart from anything else, a baby might just scare him away, not keep him captive. And if the man has not shown any interest in a commitment so far, then a pregnancy might be the last thing the relationship needs. Parenthood should be an informed choice for men and women alike.

Many couples do make the mutual decision that having a child together is something they really want to do, so if you decide that your life and relationship would be enhanced by the patter of tiny feet, then call on the Goddess to help you. On the night of the full moon light a red candle and say:

*Mother Goddess, welcome me to your ways*
*Please bring me to the mother phase.*
*Bless me with fertility*
*And send a spirit forth to me*
*By the power of mother-moon*
*Send a babe to fill my womb!*

Once you have said the incantation place your hands on your abdomen and spend a few moments visualizing yourself pregnant, healthy and happy. Then blow out the candle, making a wish for a healthy baby as you do so. Repeat the spell on the night of each full moon using the same red candle, until conception occurs. Continue with a new candle if you need to – these things can take time, so be patient.

## Be a Dark Horse

A clever temptress enhances her allure by wrapping herself in a certain amount of mystery. In these times of kiss and tell media coverage and reality TV shows it can sometimes seem as if nothing is sacred. It is as if privacy is a thing of the past and we are all expected to lay ourselves bare for the world to see. But when it comes to seduction nothing could be further from the truth; in fact, revealing too much too soon, warts and all, could send your beau running for the hills.

Mystery is a wonderful tool in the arsenal of the temptress, and discretion is sadly underrated. By its very nature, witchcraft is shrouded in mystery and intrigue. After all, the Craft is the teaching and practice of the hidden mysteries of magic, and when that is coupled with the art of seduction and falling in love a woman can appear to be very alluring and mysterious indeed. It should be said, however, that a little feminine mystique is not the same thing as outright deception, and the two should not be confused. A woman can be mysterious in a number of ways. Take for example her power to attract: people will always wonder how it is that a temptress can manage to attract the right kind of attention and turn a room full of heads wherever she goes. Her style and beauty can carry an air of mystery, in the sense that a great seductress would never let a lover see her in a mud face mask! Rather she would encourage the belief that her natural beauty needs no help. Likewise where she buys her clothes should be something that a temptress keeps to herself, for how could she maintain her unique style status if all the women she knew were buying the same outfits? Fashion and beauty secrets should remain just that – secret.

Do bear in mind that the mystery is in the mind of the observer. You need not be untruthful or deceitful. Just be slightly evasive and as charming as ever and let people's imaginations do the rest. By wrapping yourself in mystery in such simple ways, others will be puzzled and intrigued by you. They will probably want to find out more about you; they might wonder where you shop, what you read, what you do with your free time, why you are always busy, and what exactly it is that gives you that *je ne sais quoi*!

It is not difficult to be mysterious; it is simply a matter of being discreet and keeping certain things to yourself. If you want to be a successful temptress you must learn when to curb your tongue. For one thing, a very chatty individual can sometimes come across as being quite shallow, because they keep nothing hidden and we get to know everything about them, including all the mundane details of their everyday life. No one should know *everything* about you; keep some things private.

Learn to listen more than you speak, let others do the talking and keep your own counsel. Not only will this enhance your flirting skills, as I mentioned earlier, but people always assume that still waters run deep and they will be keen to fathom out your hidden depths. If someone wants to get to know you better allow them to put some effort into winning your confidences, rather than handing them your life story on the first date. Be politely evasive. If you are asked what you are doing at the weekend smile and say that you have plans, but do not elaborate. It could be that your plans involve a circus-skills or pole-dancing class, or a day in bed with a new novel and a box of chocolates, or a session as a Samaritan. It is not what you do that counts, but the sense of mystique with which you do it.

It goes without saying that you should never allow yourself to be pressured into giving out more information than you are comfortable with, including to family and friends. The more you maintain your privacy the more control you have over the flow of information that can be circulated about you. Of course there will be gossips in any social circle and nothing provokes speculation more than the sight of woman who is independent, happy and in full control of her own life and destiny. But by adding a little mystery and keeping your cards close to your chest you demonstrate your integrity, dignity and self-respect. If you keep a close guard on your private life no one will know more about you than you want them to. Try out the following tips to enhance your feminine mystique:

- Keep your own counsel and do not volunteer much information about yourself and your life. Allow your beau to unravel the layers of your personality slowly, piece by piece, in a provocative dance, revealing to him only as much as you are comfortable with.
- Start to think of yourself as a mysterious creature, a *femme fatale*, turning heads and winning the affections of the man of her choice with her fabulous charm.
- Keep a secret diary, recording all your thoughts, feelings, dreams, desires and aspirations. Seeing your life written down in a diary can help you to gain insight into any situation and it can give you a true perspective on how far you have come in your life.
- Shroud yourself in the colours of mystery and intrigue, wearing deep shades of burgundy, red, purple, grey and black. Go for a

vampish look to enhance your *femme fatale* image – be the Carmen of your own life!

- Listen to and act upon your intuition, which is a woman's greatest gift when it comes to enhancing her mystery and allure. The more you listen to your intuition the more accurate and reliable it will become. A woman's ability to 'just know' things is the core of her natural mystique, so make the very most of it.
- Learn to use a divination tool such as the crystal ball or tarot cards to further increase your sense of knowing and to deepen your insights.

## *Creature of Mystery Spell*

Perform this spell when the moon wanes to dark, which is approximately three nights after the full moon. You will need a sheer black scarf and a black candle and holder. Take these items to your dressing table at the witching hour of midnight and perform the spell before a mirror.

You will be calling upon the Celtic battle goddess Morrigan in this ritual incantation; she is a dark goddess, meaning that she is associated with secrets, mysteries, magic, glamour and enchantment. As a seductress none could match her powerful charm, and spurning her attentions would bring bad luck, misfortune and disaster. In this spell you will be asking Morrigan to help you create and maintain an aura of feminine mystique.

Sit skyclad before the mirror in total darkness. Place the black candle in the holder and light it. Look at yourself in the mirror and say:

*Here I sit in all my glory*
*Sweet mystery sings a seductive story.*

Now take the sheer black scarf and place it over your head, covering your face like a veil. Then say the incantation below three times:

*By sea, storm, wind and tree*
*Morrigan I call you, come to me.*
*Goddess of shadows and mysteries deep*
*Raven-dark Morrigan, my secrets you keep.*
*Brighten my eyes, enhance my allure,*
*Keep safe my heart, romantic and pure.*
*As I tempt and I tease, as I taunt and entice,*
*My kiss leaves him breathless, my gaze mystifies.*
*As he sees my true self; seductive and chic*
*I am strong in my power of feminine mystique.*

Remove the veil and blow out the candle. Repeat this spell as and when you feel you need to.

## Be Irresistible

A great temptress knows how to be irresistible and takes pleasure in tempting her man on a daily basis. Whether this is in the boudoir, or by giving him an accidental peak at a sexy stocking top when they are out and about, her mission is to make it virtually impossible for him to resist her. This helps to build up a high degree of sexual tension, which then snaps at the opportune moment. Most men enjoy it when the women they love make an obvious play to tempt them to do what they really want to do anyway. It puts fun and frolic into the seduction dance and, as every woman knows, laughter can be a tremendous turn-on. Add a little Wiccan magic to your irresistibility with the simple spell below.

### *Get Lucky Loadstone*

You will need a loadstone, which is a natural magnet. They are widely available quite cheaply in New Age stores and crystal shops. Place it on a windowsill in the noonday sunlight and say:

*As the trees reach for sunlight,*
*As the sunflower turns,*
*So I am a magnet*
*And my irresistibility burns!*

Leave it in place and then in the evening put it into the light of the moon and say:

*As the moon pulls the tides*
*And shines bright in the night*
*So my magnetism sparkles*
*And men are drawn to my light!*

Your loadstone will now be fully charged with solar and lunar energies, so carry it with you in a pocket or purse to become more irresistible. Recharge it in sunlight and moonlight once every month to maintain its power and be sure to carry it with you on all your dates.

## Astral Lovers

There might be times when you and your lover cannot be together physically and you are missing him like crazy. A little witchery can help to ease the yearnings. Witches believe in the astral plane, which is an alternative dimension to the Earth plane. This is where elementals reside, and where visualizations, meditations and dreams take place. Some people believe that they can meet up with loved ones, both living and dead, on the astral plane during their sleep. So if you are missing your true love try the following ritual to bring him into your dreams.

### *Dream Lover*

First make a few preparations. Have a sweet-scented bath and put on your sexiest lingerie or nightwear. Scent your pillow with your lover's favourite fragrance so that you can recall the scent of him as you sleep. Put a photograph of him by the bed so that you see his face just before your drop off to sleep. Leave the curtains open a little so that the moonlight can spill into the room and then stand at the window and address your incantation to the night sky.

*Mother moon, mother moon, bright orb of the sky*
*Bring together my lover and me.*
*So much do I miss him, I long for his kiss*
*Reunite us in dreamtime, together in bliss!*
*Guide us forth in our sleep to the astral plane*
*Bring my lover to me as I call out his name.*

Say your lover's name out loud three times and then get into bed and whisper his name until you fall asleep. You should dream of your man, and he of you, within the next three nights.

*Wear a soothing eye mask such as one fragranced with lavender, to help you get a restful night of beauty sleep and to help prevent puffy eyes the following day.*

CHAPTER 9

# The Great Seduction

Having sex, whether it is for the first time or over the long period of a committed relationship, should always be a magical experience. It should be enjoyable, romantic, sensual, passionate and provocative. Men like to be seduced, just as much as women, and they are turned on by the fact that their partner has taken control of the situation. Young men might even fantasize about an older woman taking them in hand and becoming a sexual mentor. This goes back to what was said earlier about men having been introduced to the idea of woman as temptress from a relatively young age.

An effective seduction is like a slow, sensuous dance. Nothing is rushed, no clocks are watched and both parties behave as if time has stood still, just for them. Simply put, seduction takes as long as it takes and racing to the finish line is not seductive, and it can even be a turn off.

Lots of women fantasize about seduction; it is a common theme in erotic fiction, with writers creating strong powerful heroes to seduce fresh young girls from their virgin state. These heroes tend to be experienced in both life and love. They might be rich and powerful and they usually exhibit a certain degree of arrogance and egotism; they might even be dangerous. But what they all have in common is that they know beyond the shadow of a doubt that they will eventually get the girl and win the prize. With such certain knowledge they can afford to take their time, leading the young heroine a merry dance along the way! The artful seducer battles through all of her defences, ignores her half-hearted objections and proceeds to bring the affair to its natural climax. This type of seductive theme is by no means new; it even appears in the plot lines of classic literature too – take for example young Tess Durbeyfield being expertly seduced by the rakish Alec D'Urberville, or the gypsy Heathcliff wooing Cathy on the Yorkshire moors. The art of seduction is as old as the hills, and it is a very useful skill to have.

## In the Mood

The great seduction takes time and effort, and you will need to gear yourself up for the event. Many women complain that their lover expects to turn them on like a switch and that they seem to have no idea that there is work involved. Of course if a woman is faking orgasms then she is just as much to blame as he is, for she is misleading him into thinking that he is making all the right moves. It has to be said, too, that for men the seduction usually begins in the bedroom; for women it needs to begin much earlier and most of us like to be wooed and romanced before we even get to the bedroom!

It must also be said that the libido does fluctuate for both men and women. There will be times when you cannot get enough sex, and others when the very thought of an intimate liaison is too much effort and you would rather have a nice glass of wine and some chocolate. A woman's menstrual cycle has a profound effect on her libido; she is programmed to feel more sexual when she is at her most fertile – this is nature's way of propagating the species. It can also mean that the female libido slumps at a certain stage in her cycle, which is perfectly natural. Even a Wiccan temptress cannot be super-sexy all the time.

Having said that, sometimes all you need is a bit of a sexual boost and there are things that you can do to kick start your libido and get you in the mood for love. Try reading erotic fiction. It need not be soft porn – unless you want it to be. It might be a steamy historical romance or a family saga. Or try erotic fiction which is written by women and is designed to turn them on; the lingerie giant Agent Provocateur produces some excellent volumes which are beautifully covered and would make an elegant and discreet addition to any woman's boudoir. They are small enough to fit into a handbag too, so you could boost your libido on the commute home from work and be ready for your lover as soon as you walk in the door!

Fantasizing is another great way to rev up your love motor. Think about the last time you made love with your partner. Think about what he did to you, how he made you feel, and the sweet words he whispered. Think of your very first love or an old flame. Or go with a full fantasy and imagine having hot and steamy sex with your favourite actor. Who is your dream man? What would your ultimate scenario of seduction be? Picture it in your mind casting yourself as the sultry heroine and your libido is likely to respond in kind.

As I said earlier women can generally be turned on by romance. We like to be wooed, and a romantic event can be a great trigger to the sex drive so watch some romantic films with strong, chivalrous leading men to trick your body into anticipating a liaison. Light a few scented candles, pour a glass of wine, have some chocolates at the ready, then lie back and allow yourself to be wooed by your chosen hero. You are likely to be all the more responsive to your lover if your head is full of romantic Byronic heroes or knights in armour.

Another way to raise your body's sex drive and get in the mood is to wear your sexiest lingerie. When you look sexy, you will feel sexy and when you feel sexy you will behave in a more seductive and provocative manner. Wander around the house in your skimpiest underwear and tallest heels and then see how long you can keep your thoughts off sex! These are all great ways to get in the mood for love making if your libido is temporarily letting you down. And if your man is not known for his patience such tricks can give you a head start so that you gain as much enjoyment from the liaison as he does. Take a few moments now and think about what your own triggers are and how you could use them to enhance your personal pleasure and your relationship.

## Who's Seducing Whom?

While love making might be a mutual engagement the initial seduction usually requires lovers to take on one of two roles: the seducer or the seduced. This basically means that one person is initiating a sexual encounter while the other is responding. A great seduction is a power play, where one person takes charge of the initiation, timing, pacing and location of the liaison, gently leading their love interest along the path of bliss, while the other person is content to be led. Anyone can be a seducer, just as anyone can find themselves being seduced. The key is to find out who is playing which role – and they are not gender specific – and then act accordingly. Be aware, too, that the roles can switch, even within the same seduction. So if he initiated the seduction then perhaps it is time to return the favour!

### *If You Want Him to Seduce You*

- Appeal to his masculinity by playing up your femininity. Wear girly outfits in feminine colours such as pink, peach, violet and white. Wear pretty, feminine lingerie in chiffon and lace. Virginal white is always a winner if you want him to seduce you and take the lead.
- Wear shoes with a low heel to ensure that he is taller than you. Again this will bring out his protective masculine instincts and he will want to look after you and lead the way.
- Wear a soft, floral fragrance to further increase your femininity and apply a little make-up to enhance your natural allure. Make the most of your figure without drawing attention to obvious areas – think demure. Then act in a soft, feminine manner. Play the shy girl. Be the coquette and wait for him to kiss you.

## If You Want to be the Seductress

- Make the most of your inner siren by dressing to thrill. Power colours such as black and red are perfect for the seductress. Add a touch of gold or even a dash of purple to give your look regal authority.
- Wear sexy, racy lingerie in satin, silk and even velvet. Pick jewel-like colours and structured pieces to make the very most of your assets. Push up bras, basques and stockings will all help to put you in the driving seat.
- Wear sky high heels, figure-hugging clothing and vampish make-up, together with a musky, woody, 'come hither' fragrance. But do not overdo it. Your aim is to look so sexy it hurts, yet still retain a classic sophistication; if you have edged into dominatrix mode then you have gone too far and are more likely to scare him than seduce him.

## Hints That He Wants to be Seduced

Sex is a great form of exercise and when a man takes the dominant role he uses up a lot of energy, so he might like to take things easy once in a while by simply lying back and enjoying it. If this is the case his body language will send out subtle signs so keep your eyes peeled for these hints that he wants you to seduce him:

- His kisses will be softer and more tentative and he might even pull back slightly, inviting you to kiss him, rather than the other way around.
- He is more likely to keep his hands to himself, or maybe to let them rest on your waist or hips in a relaxed, non-sexual manner. At the same time his lower body might turn towards you slightly or he might subtly move his hips towards you, encouraging you to engage! Basically his body is screaming at you to take the initiative and he wants to be touched by loving hands.

- If he leans right back, or lies on his back and throws his arms out slightly to the side then he is inviting you to be the dominant one, as such a motion is an ancient battle and sporting gesture of submission! Simply put, he is yielding to your feminine power.

## Seductive Enchantments

No matter who chooses to take on the dominant role of seducer a woman can enhance all her encounters with a little magic and witchery. Witchcraft has been used for centuries as a way of keeping relationships hot and steamy and there are a wide range of traditional spells and rituals to choose from. In the past the village wise woman would have been called upon to help with a myriad of sexual problems and frustrations, from impotence and infertility to winning back an old lover and increasing one's attractiveness.

Having a little magic on your side could help you to turn an ordinary encounter into a truly enchanting one. Spells can also help you to overcome sexual nerves, shyness and embarrassment. Few of us are fortunate enough to look like an air brushed super-model when in the buff so a little extra help to radiate your inner goddess and siren self can only be a good thing. In view of this there follows a selection of rituals which should help to increase the glamour and enchantment of your more intimate moments.

### *Casting a Glamour Spell*

A glamour spell is a magical illusion which can subtly alter how others perceive you and also how you perceive yourself. It could even be said to be cosmic air-brushing. In essence it is a way of giving your confidence a magical boost, of putting your best face forward so to speak, and radiating your inner goddess out into the world. When you have a glamour spell on your side you will feel more confident, alluring, and enigmatic and you will act accordingly, leading others to see you in this way, which in turn reinforces the glamour spell. By casting a glamorie as it is known, you are in fact taking charge of your image and of how your lover sees you. It is a very simple ruse, but it is also powerfully effective and a traditional tool of the magical temptress.

## *Swan Song Glamour Ritual*

On the night of the full moon leave a silver or glass bowl full of spring water outside to soak up the magical moonbeams. Take it indoors at dawn, before the sun is fully risen. Add three tablespoons of rose water and the petals of three red or pink roses, preferably taken from your own garden. On the evening of your planned seduction take the glamour potion into the bathroom along with a large white feather. Run a warm bath and light a few candles. Then stand naked and use the feather to brush the potion all over your face and body, making sure your skin is evenly covered. As you do so say the following incantation three times:

*A sacred swan-maid I would be*
*And so I cast this glamorie.*
*When my lover comes to me*
*Let him see my goddess beauty*
*And as I move with swan-like grace*
*Let my true love's heartbeat race*
*And as we couple, one on one*
*Let him know my inner swan,*
*Then let him rest in deep amour*
*Beguiled by my sweet allure!*

Add the remainder of the potion to your bath, and you will know that you are enveloped in the spell of swan-like glamour.

## *Queen of the Night*

To dispel any anxiety, embarrassment or shyness before it takes hold of you, cast this simple spell as you prepare for your liaison.

It will help you to become a goddess incarnate and a true queen of the night. All you need is a stick of night queen incense which is available from New Age stores. Prepare for your night of fun and frolic by wearing a sexy ensemble and applying your make-up, styling your hair, etc. When you are ready light the incense and use it like a pencil to draw an archway slightly larger than yourself in the air before you. Step through the smoky arch and say:

*Through the smoke and into the light*
*So I become Queen of the Night.*
*None can hold a candle to me*
*When I set my inner siren free.*
*Goddess I am and Goddess will be*
*Sweet goddess-love flows through me!*

Repeat the procedure until you have stepped through the smoke and said the incantation three times in all, then place the incense in a suitable holder on your love altar and allow it to burn down naturally. The spell is complete.

## Lunar Love Potion

What better way to begin a night of seduction than by handing your beau a love potion made by your own fair hands as soon as he walks through the door? When people think of love spells and rituals the idea of a love potion usually springs immediately to mind. There is something very romantic about making and sharing a love potion. It stirs the imagination, bringing images of Arthurian lovers to mind. Potions are easy to make and simple to use.

About half an hour before your lover is due to arrive open a bottle of red wine; buy the best that you can afford. Now add three drops of Cherry Plum Bach Flower Remedy for romance and arousal, three drops of Oak Bach Flower Remedy for stamina, and one drop of pure vanilla essence for its aphrodisiac qualities. Cover the neck of the bottle and give the wine a gentle shake, then holding the bottle firmly say:

*Gracious Goddess, infuse this potion with your gifts of love, passion and ardour. Let it serve as an aphrodisiac for my lover and me. So mote it be.*

Allow the wine to breath for about fifteen minutes then pour out two glasses and hold them up, presenting them to the moon – you can do this out of doors or through a window. Now say:

*I offer up this gift to share*
*Bestow your magic through the air.*
*Mother moon, lover's friend*
*To this potion your power lend.*
*Tonight, this boon I ask you send:*
*A night of passion without end*
*So mote it be.*

When your lover arrives hand him the potion with a kiss to seal the spell and let the enchanted wine perform its magic!

## Hot Couple Candle Spell

In a long-term relationship the passion can dissipate over time. Although magic can help to keep a relationship hot and healthy it is no substitute for effort. This means that you need to make time for one another and make a commitment not to take your relationship for granted. Too many relationships fizzle out due to neglect and this is when an affair becomes a real danger. So to enhance your own personal efforts cast the following spell to help keep your relationship hot.

You will need a large red pillar candle and a suitable holder. Try to choose something pretty, as it will be a decorative addition to your boudoir. If you like you can use a scented candle but that is not essential. Once you have your candle use a sharp knife or athame to carve your name and the name of your partner on it. Then carve a love heart to represent the emotional attachment to one another. Next, anoint the candle with sunflower oil to represent the heat and passion of your sex life and to stir up the attraction. Finally, hold it and say this incantation below:

*This candle bearing both our names*
*Rekindles passion in its flames.*
*Renew the lust, renew the heat*
*Renew our bond between the sheets.*
*I burn for him, he burns for me*
*Together in fidelity.*
*Push the boundaries, spice it up*
*Renew the flame and stir the blood.*
*Together in sweet harmony*
*In perfect love, so mote it be.*

Place the candle in the holder and keep it in the boudoir on your love altar. Light it and let it burn for a few minutes each day and especially when you make love. Once the candle has burnt away, replace it and repeat the spell.

## Sexy Treasure Hunt

Lead your man a merry dance by creating a sexy treasure hunt for him to follow. This is a great way to surprise him on a special occasion such as Valentine's Day or on his birthday. You will need to obtain as many small, sexy gifts as you have rooms in your house. They need not be expensive; think about using chocolate hearts, condoms, massage oil or edible body paint. Leave a small gift in each room, along with a hand-written clue to send him on to the next location. If you do not want to leave gifts then leave discarded items of your clothing with the clues instead. Write out your favourite love poems and leave these with the clues too to add a sense of romance. Then just before your man is due home, illuminate the house with candles, leave a sexy pair of knickers by the door so that he will see them when he comes in and go and dress in your sexiest lingerie and wait for him in the bedroom.

This should be the last room he comes to. Sit quietly and listen as he moves through the house discovering the gifts and following the clues to the greatest treasure of all – you! This is great fun and it will be something the two of you will always remember.

## Dressing up for Love

Dressing up for love making is a good way to create an added zing in a long-term relationship, but before your mind recoils in embarrassment at the idea of a French maid's outfit, bear in mind that there is more to dressing up than tacky costumes and role play. Often the simplest thing can be very seductive: a pair of satin gloves in which you stroke your lover's skin, a feather boa to tickle his fancy, a racy basque, a chain-mail top over a leather bodice. If he knows of your Wiccan ways try wearing a black witch's cloak with nothing on underneath. Add a sexy black feather eye mask to increase the mystique. Use simple sexy touches which can be mixed in with ordinary clothes then play a demure game of 'Sexy? This old thing? Do you really think so?'

## Private Dancer

Exotic and erotic dancing has long been used as a tool of seduction and although modern night clubs might like to take all the credit, sexy dancing is by no means new. Nor is nudity compulsory – a woman can be just as seductive, if not more so, in a carefully planned dance costume. The important thing is that she feels comfortable and confident, as self-conscious fidgeting is not sexy!

Some years ago I worked in a night club as a dancing barmaid. We had to wear blue leotards and tutus and although the dancing was far from raunchy, the young men who frequented the club would flock to see us and we would often go home with an armful of red roses which the lads had bought for us. It was harmless, flirtatious fun, but it did teach me that men respond to a visual cue and that this is often the best way to spark their interest. It does not take much for a woman to be treated like a sex-goddess: a little bit of grace, a lot of dignity, a charming smile and some flattering lighting and you can have them eating out of your hand in no time.

Dancing has to be one of the easiest ways to get a man's attention. Centuries ago dance was used as a way of honouring and communing with divinity, and the great temples would house virgins – girls who danced for their gods for the good of the people. Even today witches use dance as a way of raising power for their rituals and honouring the Goddess.

Dancing is the easiest way to make you feel like a goddess and to arouse men – that is why the Puritans banned it! It is fantastic exercise and it can be great fun too. It is certainly a far more pleasurable experience than spending hours on the treadmill. Dancing with a man is basically vertical foreplay, and a man who can dance well is a huge turn-on for most women. One only has to think of the success of Patrick Swayze in the film *Dirty Dancing*, or Michael Flatley following *Riverdance*, and later *Lord of the Dance*, to see that this is true. And the more limber his hips the more lascivious and wanton we are a liable to become! Recall the thousands of screaming girls at an Elvis Presley concert or, in more recent years, at a Chippendales concert during the 1980s and early 1990s.

Dancing is not without controversy however, and even classical ballet, now considered to be the height of culture and sophistication, caused an outcry at the first appearance of the tutu, which was considered to be obscene! Even today there might be demonstrations at the opening of a new 'gentlemen's club' – although it must be said that pole dancing has become far more mainstream and accepted than it was just ten years ago. Now pole-dancing work-out classes are available to women who want a fun way to tone up and keep in shape. There are even poles available to erect in your own home.

Dancing erotically for your partner is a great way to turn him on and to keep him faithful – why would he stray when he has his own sexy, private dancer at home? There are many ways in which you can learn to dance: take up a class, put on some music and teach yourself, learn from the stars by watching the music videos of Britney Spears or Shakira, or buy a dance work-out – I can personally recommend *Amira's Bellydance 101* from New World Music, which is fantastic fun and will soon have you bopping with the best of them. Or try the *New York Ballet Work-Out*, which is available from most shops.

Once you have mastered your chosen dance, light some candles, play some music, put on something sexy and dance for your beau; imagine that you are a gypsy temptress dancing around the camp fire with a beribboned tambourine, or a sultry Eastern Princess dancing for her sultan.

## Temptress Tip

*When indulging in erotic dance apply a shimmering body bronzer to hide a multitude of sins such as cellulite and stretch marks. Then apply a thin line of Vaseline up the centre of your legs and down the front of your arms to make you appear taller and more willowy. Dance in candlelight for the most flattering effect.*

## Siren Secret

*Magical seduction should help to take all the stress out of sexual encounters and increase the fun. It will also give you a witchy edge over the competition! It will help to keep your relationship hot and steamy too. To be a great seductress you must first learn to think of yourself as a great seductress and then act accordingly. Try not to be shy – any man would be lucky to be with you, even for a moment, you mystifying, tantalizing, hip-shimmying vixen!*

CHAPTER 10

# The One That Got Away

There is always one who gets away – the man who was too strong and independent to be landed, too free spirited, but also, infuriatingly, too gorgeous to forget! He is the old flame your mind conjures up when your love life is flagging, the one you dream about, fantasize about, and maybe even write poetry about. He is the one you remember when you look up at the stars and, gazing at the moon, whisper a secret goodnight to. He is the one you would have baked cakes for, kept house for. However, there is likely to be a good reason why he got away in the first place.

That being the case, why does he still hold such power over you? Why, perhaps many years later, do your thoughts still turn to him, why do you relive all the things you did together, all the conversations you ever had with him, all the things you wish you had said and done together?

It is possible that women have a stronger affinity with the past than men do. It is thought that while men might fall in love much faster than we do, women tend to love longer, harbouring emotional ties months, even years after a relationship has fizzled out. Men may tend to move on more quickly after a romantic disappointment, dating someone else within a relatively short period of time. Of course, I am generalizing here, and I am in no way implying that all men are shallow and fickle. Perhaps they are simple more pragmatic and resilient, not to mention biologically programmed to spread their seed and propagate the species. And some men do take a long time to get over a difficult break up.

Most women have a very romantic soul; and we are often accused of being ruled by our emotions rather than by our intellect. There may well be some truth in this, and it can lead us to view people and situations through rose-tinted glasses. I have certainly been guilty of this myself in the past. While it would be wonderful if every woman's life resembled a romantic novel, unfortunately life is not always willing to oblige! But we learn the most useful lessons from the challenges we face.

This rose-tinted outlook on life can lead us to romanticize a long-dead relationship, turning the lost lover into the ultimate romantic hero and the answer to all of our feminine dreams. Of course the reality is that he probably was not anything like that. And, as I have said, there is usually a reason why the relationship did not work out, or did not even get off the ground. Usually when we reminisce we look back on all the good times and ignore the bad. The one that got away has power over you because you forget his faults, and the reason why he is not with you now. If you are not currently together, then perhaps it was just not meant to be. By over-romanticizing him and your past with him, you are in effect giving him all of your power and projecting your personal happiness on to a fantasy reunion and the whim of fate. This can be very damaging to your self-esteem if fate does not oblige.

Having said that I am fully aware that some people may simply lose touch and drift apart. Circumstances change: people move house, leave town, emigrate and change careers, and so on, making it very easy to mislay an old friend. The success of websites such as Friends Reunited is proof of this, and many an old flame has been rekindled under the guise of catching up with an old acquaintance. The simple fact of the matter is that the only way to get beyond the 'if only' feeling is to take the bull by the horns and be proactive. This is the only way to find out once and for all if what could have been will ever be in reality. The outcome might not be what you wanted or expected, but at least you will be able to move on with your life. So if you want him, go out and get him! But before you do, there are one or two points to bear in mind. You must be prepared to take the full consequences of your actions, which means that:

- You must be prepared for the fact that he might reject you totally, and without sparing a thought for your feelings.
- You must also be prepared to do the honourable thing and bow out gracefully if you discover that he is with someone else. A Wiccan temptress has no need to poach someone else's man. Walk away with dignity and get on with your life.
- If he is single and interested in starting up a relationship with you then you must be prepared to accept him unconditionally as the man he is now, not the man you knew before. People and circumstances change. It is unlikely that anyone will get past the age of thirty without acquiring some sort of emotional or circumstantial baggage – he might have children, or a demanding career, or the ex-wife from hell. Whatever his baggage may be you must accept it without recrimination and he of course must do the same with regard to your own life changes.

If you are fully prepared to accept the possibility of one of these scenarios then it is time for you to stop dreaming and start scheming – in the nicest possible way, of course!

## Tracking Him Down

In order to have any chance at all of winning back your old beau you first need to track him down. It can be nerve wracking and at the same time very exciting. Whatever the outcome, whether you get back together or not, the fact remains that you are taking your heart on a high-risk adventure without a safety net, so bear in mind that there are no guarantees that you will emerge unscathed.

There will be sleepless nights, day-dreaming, adrenalin rushes and possibly even a mild panic attack each time the phone rings or you have an email.

It is vitally important therefore that you set up guards around yourself to protect you from any unforeseen fallout. Remember that there is a reason it did not work before, and in searching him out you are effectively giving him the opportunity to hurt you all over again. And he might not want you to come looking for him; not all men will be flattered by your attentions. So keep as much of the power to yourself as you can; by this I mean that it is in your own interests to keep your longing for him secret until you are more sure of his feelings towards to you. Keeping this in mind it is by far the best approach to orchestrate a chance meeting, you can always come clean at a later date. If you know where he lives, works, or goes with his friends, then this will be easy. If not try browsing the appropriate websites to see it he is posted, and drop him a friendly email. Or take a look at the electoral role. If all else fails you could hire a private detective to track him down for you. This is not nearly as expensive as you might imagine and such people are well used to locating old friends and long-lost lovers, so your story will probably be familiar to them.

Bear in mind that you should only bump into your old flame once or twice. If he gives no indication of wanting to become reacquainted then you must walk away with dignity – anything else is known as stalking. Maintain your self-respect at all times.

## *Scry for Him*

To help set the universal ball rolling you could scry for your old beau's approximate location using a pendulum and a map of the area. First determine which way your pendulum swings for yes and no answers by asking it a question to which you know the answer is yes, followed by one to which you know the answer is no. Once you have discovered how your pendulum swings out its answers, hold it still over a map of the local area. Slowly move the pendulum around the map saying, '(Name) lives here?' Once you have your answer you can then move on to the next stage.

Light a tea-light and place it in an appropriate holder, then write the full name and date of birth (if known) of the person you wish to get back in touch with on a small slip of paper. Burn the spell paper in the tea light flame while saying the incantation:

*(Name) come to me,*
*By this spell I summon thee.*
*Cross the universe to my side*
*And heal the breech of time's divide.*

Repeat the spell daily until you become aware of your old flame's location and current circumstances.

## Play It Cool

If you locate your old flame and, on making a few discreet enquiries, it turns out that he is single and looking for love, this is your cue to get serious. Orchestrate or arrange a meeting with him. It should be during the day if at all possible; in this way you will keep things light and friendly – there should be no hint at this very early stage that you have romance on your mind. Sound him out a bit before your bare your soul! Make an effort to look fantastic, but in a casual way. Do not try too hard, as you do not want to seem desperate, so keep your love-light on a low setting. Think demure allure, flirty girly, not rampant sex goddess. You can always introduce him to that aspect of your character at a later date if the relationship gets going.

Guard your heart and be discreet. Do not bolster his ego by telling him that you have never got over him or that you cannot stop thinking about him. Do not beg him for another chance. Play it cool – be friendly and fun. Let him know that it is great to see him again, but then let him do the work. Remember, men chase, women choose. You have already made your choice clear; now you need to step back and let him chase you. Use the spells below to help reel him in and to give you a magical edge.

## *Let the Angels Set You Up!*

Ask the angels to help with your plans and to give you a little celestial help in the following way. Go to your love altar and take a notepad and pen and a pink candle. Carve the name of your old flame into the pink candle, place it in a suitable holder, and then light it and say:

*Angels I call you; please light the way.*
*Assist the reunion I ask for this day.*
*This candle burns brightly; it spells out a name.*
*Please guide this man to me, along lover's lane!*

As the candle burns, write a letter to your guardian angel and explain why you are asking for this reunion to take place. Ask that the angels assist you and that they create the opportunity for you to meet up with your old flame and renew your friendship if this is for the highest good of both parties. Sign and date the letter, then burn it in the candle flame, dropping it into a heat-proof bowl to burn away. Allow the pink candle to burn naturally.

## *Reel Him In*

Encourage your old beau to take a second bite of the apple by casting this spell of goddess-attraction to reel him in. At your love altar light a tea-light and a stick of your favourite incense. Place them in appropriate holders and settle down to focus on the flame of the tea-light. Picture the face of your old flame and begin to chant the following goddess incantation:

*Powers of attraction in which I believe*
*Venus, Diana, Aphrodite and Eve*
*Queens of the four realms, lend me your charms*
*By witchcraft I call him into my arms!*

Continue to chant for as long as you remain focused. Make sure that you repeat the incantation at least nine times. Repeat the spell each week on a Friday evening, which is the day of love and passion.

## Let Him Go

As I have said, locating someone from your past is not always going to bring about a happy ending. It could be that all your time, effort and hard work reveal that your old flame is already involved with someone else or not interested. The heartache which follows can be acute. But now is the time to demonstrate your honour, integrity and strength of character by walking away with your head held high. People move on and you should not blame him for doing just that and getting on with things. He did not ask you to track him down or pin all your hopes and dreams on him. Be grateful for the time you did have together and move on. This is of course much easier said than done. If you have set your heart on something and have spent time pursuing it then it is natural to be shattered when it does not turn out as you had hoped. It is mortifying to set your cap at someone and have them totally ignore it. Your heart will be bruised, but the deepest wound is more likely to be to your pride. By all means have a brief rant, cry into your pillow if needs be, but ultimately you must accept that the time has come to let him go once and for all. You must also assume that he is happy. If he is settled in a state of domestic bliss, do not begin to imagine cracks in his relationship; you could then become the home wrecker who puts the cracks there. Presumably you care deeply for this man or you would not have taken the trouble to find him. That being the case, find it in your heart to be glad that he has found happiness and have the grace to wish him well.

Take comfort in the knowledge that you did all that you could to bring a relationship with this man into being but it simply was not meant to be. The universe has bigger and better plans for you. In the meantime work these spells to apply a magical salve to the wound.

### *Let Him Go Spell*

For this you will need to obtain a helium balloon; try to pick a heart-shaped one if you can. Take it to your love altar and dab a little lavender essential oil on to it to represent healing. Then write your old flame's name on a slip of paper and copy the following incantation beneath it:

*I searched for you across land and sea*
*But no more do you dream of me;*
*Another fills your heart and soul.*
*I wish you well and let you go.*

Sign the slip and tie it to the ribbon of the balloon. Then take the balloon outside, repeat the incantation once more and let it go as soon as you feel ready. Watch it drift away in the knowledge that you are now entering a new phase of your life.

### Melt the Pain

The second spell uses the calming energies of water. Soon after your disappointment take an ice cube from the freezer and hold it to your skin over your heart. Feel the first bite of the icy chill, which represents the pain and emotional numbness you are likely to be feeling. Take some time to think over your disappointment and allow the ice to slowly melt, representing your tears. As the water drips it washes away the pain of the disappointment. Feel free to cry and grieve as the ice melts. When you feel calmer, put the ice in a bowl and let it continue to melt, then pour the healing water into the earth to further neutralize your pain.

## The End of the Road

All relationships end; whether by death, divorce, deceit or general deterioration, all eventually reach a conclusion. But endings, like beginnings, are all a part of the natural cycle of life.

The fact that women tend to live longer than men means that even if you are lucky enough to have a long marriage, there is still a chance that you will become a single woman once more at some point in the future.

The death of any relationship is a bereavement. Although it is natural for a relationship to draw to a close eventually this does not make the event any easier to deal with, particularly if you feel that you had no say in the matter and your partner was taken away from you by circumstance or death. In the bigger picture it could be a sign that you are about to move into a new phase in your life; that you have grown as an individual and are ready for a fresh challenge. It could also be that your partner was around to teach you a very specific life lesson; once you have learned this lesson his job is done and the universe may well take him away to complete his own journey and life path, leaving you free to carry your new-found wisdom on to the new stage of your life. While it might be difficult to find anything spiritual in a bad break-up the fact is that the only way to deal with it is to grieve and then move on. Eventually you will feel ready to embrace your life as a single woman, and when that happens, you will need the following spell.

## *Single Hot Witch Spell!*

This is an adaptation of the earlier attraction spell and it is designed for single women who want to be more attractive in general, rather than to attract someone in particular.

On a red candle carve the names of Venus, Diana, Aphrodite and Eve. Set the candle in a holder on your love altar and light it. Now focus on the flame and envisage yourself as a confident, single witch, having fun and enjoying your liberty. When you are ready, light the candle and repeat this incantation three times.

*Powers of attraction in which I believe*
*Venus, Diana, Aphrodite and Eve*
*I am a seductress, enchantress and queen.*
*No man can resist me; I am ready to be seen*
*By powers of beauty in which I believe,*
*By Venus, Diana, Aphrodite and Eve,*
*I cast this spell, true love to know*
*As I will, it shall be so!*

Allow the candle to burn for five minutes then blow it out. Light it and repeat the incantation each night, allowing the candle to burn for five minutes a night until it is gone. Repeat the whole spell whenever you feel that your powers of attraction need a lift.

## Temptress Tip

*To help jog an old flame's memory make sure you wear the same perfume you used to wear when you were first together. This will set his mind to reminiscing and will remind him of all that he has been missing!*

## Siren Secret

*Although it is quite natural to think of old flames from time to time, if you are making a habit of drooling over men from your past then you need to ask yourself why. A brief fixation on a certain special someone is one thing; working your way through your little black book is quite another!*

*Sometimes we fantasize because a fantasy allows us to experience the essence of love and romance without the danger of being hurt or rejected. Again, for a brief period this is fine and a healthy way of beginning to move on following a bad break-up. It is a sign that your thoughts at least are turning towards love and relationships again. Hiding behind one fantasy after another, however, is actually an indication that you are avoiding love rather than looking for it, as you might at first suppose. By all means play the old records and reminisce, but do make sure that you remain open minded about the new loves which life can offer you.*

CHAPTER 11

# *Brief Encounters*

There may be times in a woman's life when she is not in a relationship. There are, however, degrees of singleness, and as I have said being single does not necessarily mean that a woman is without male companionship and attention. Nor does it imply that she is totally celibate and left on the shelf or that she is sleeping around. These are the extreme stereotypes of the single woman.

Every woman will be single in her own way; while some embrace their footloose and fancy-free status, celebrating with a string of recreational sex partners, others take the high ground and choose celibacy, which is not without its merits. Then there is always the middle ground: the together-apart relationship or even the platonic male friend. We will be exploring all of these options in this chapter, for as a single hot temptress you have the freedom of choice which married women are conventionally denied.

Sexual freedom is one of the greatest gifts of the Goddess, and a woman can experience great sexual pleasure these days without a wedding ring to weigh her down or cramp her style. If you believe in soul mates then it is unlikely – though not impossible – that you will meet him on your first trip around the block, going on to live happily ever after. And women have oats to sow, just as men do. It is better for the long-term relationship that both partners have seen something of life before they choose to settle down. Your wings should not be clipped before you have had a chance to test them. Providing that you are taking your personal safety seriously there is no reason why you should not make an active search for your ideal partner. It is your body after all, and you have the right to share it with whomever you please, or to keep it entirely to yourself.

On that note let us begin our exploration of the single girl's life by taking a look at the stereotypical role society carves out for her.

## Single and Celibate

Even in these modern times people tend to equate being single with being celibate, and celibacy still has a certain stigma attached to it. I believe that this goes back to the Victorian age and before, when girls lived in fear of becoming an old maid, and could genuinely think of nothing more depressing than being passed over by all the eligible young men and remaining unmarried. Although thankfully times have changed and marriage need not be every woman's highest aspiration, something of this attitude still survives in the stigma surrounding celibacy.

Single celibate girls are usually viewed in two ways: either with a certain amount of misplaced pity as in 'the poor girl can't get a man'; and secondly as a huge threat to other women, who wrongly assume that celibacy is synonymous with desperation. These women are aware that prolonged celibacy is similar to a second virginity and so men will be challenged and intrigued! A third school of thought assumes that a single girl must be a lesbian. Such assumptions are insulting, and I would like to offer a different and more empowering view of celibacy – one which is based upon feminine independence and self-respect.

It is my belief that female celibacy is akin to the ancient view of virginity in that a woman is beholden to no man. In this sense celibacy is basically a second virginity and it could be viewed as the ultimate in feminine independence: here is a woman who actively chooses to withhold her sexual favours from mankind. Celibacy is not without its merits.

In making the decision to be celibate a woman is effectively placing herself on something like a pedestal – not in an egotistical sense, but in order to gain time and space to herself so that she can re-evaluate what she wants from life and love. This pedestal also gives her a marvellous vantage point from which she can observe who and what is out there – all the better to make her move when she is ready to get back in the game. And being on a pedestal makes men perceive her as an unreachable, unattainable temptress. In this sense a vow of celibacy is a very shrewd manoeuvre!

In addition, by remaining celibate for any length of time a woman is far less likely to settle for second best or to spend intimate time with someone she does not really want nor have any genuine affection for. So celibacy helps her to become more objective in identifying what she wants, at the same time increasing her sense of self-worth and self-respect. Celibacy can also give someone the time and space they need to recover from a romantic trauma. This is true for both sexes of course.

Human nature being what it is we often find ourselves wanting what we cannot have, and the pedestal of celibacy can actually make someone seem even more desirable. In fact a woman who is open about her celibate status is likely to receive even more masculine attention than other, sexually available women, as men will try to woo her off the pedestal. Do not expect other women to like you for this! And if someone finally does woo her back into the game of flirtation and love, at least both parties will know that it is for the right reasons and is not just a case of passing a bit of time.

So celibacy need not be a bad thing and it certainly does not mean that a woman has been left on the shelf. Nor does it make her any less of a temptress, for she can still turn heads and enjoy attention. When she is ready to dip her toe in the water again there are one or two options open to her which will allow her to maintain her single status and independence.

## Booty Calls

Booty calls were in existence long before All Saints started singing about them! Basically, they involve no-strings-attached recreational sex with a man you know well and whom you trust completely. Relationship etiquette states that he must of course be entirely single when you call to ask him for a favour. If he has a girlfriend then he is absolutely off limits. Prime booty callers are generally single men who are very free spirited and do not really want to be tied down. Safe sex is a must – how do you know that you are his only midnight caller? A very good male friend whom you have occasionally woken up next to is also a kind of booty call, though usually of a more spontaneous variety.

In any booty call relationship it is essential that the boundaries are absolutely clear; if you find yourself day dreaming about him or are jealous of the other women in his life then you are developing a romantic attachment to him, which may not be what he wants, nor is it likely to be in your own best interests. Booty calls are safer than one-night stands and they can be a great boost to your ego after a romantic disappointment. Just make sure that such a relationship is by mutual agreement and you are not just stringing some poor man along.

## Independent Lovers

This is a situation in which some mature people find themselves. It is a sensible option if you do not want to live with someone but still want the security of a committed relationship. This is how it usually works: you live alone and he lives alone, but you frequently get together for dates, days out, dinners and holidays. While you choose not to live together or marry, your commitment to one another is undeniable. You are faithful to each other sexually and you are considered to be an item among your peers. This scenario is perfect for those people who need their own space and like to have time to themselves. It is not the best option for those who have jealousy or co-dependency issues to deal with, as the time spent apart would drive you mad! But if you are free spirited and independent it could give you the romance and companionship you want without chipping away at your autonomy. It is the very best of both worlds, and because you will not be living in each other's pockets the thrill and romance are likely to last much longer. You are also likely to be more appreciative of one another during the times you are together.

## Platonic Male Friend

This option has all the benefits of being an independent lover but without the sex. A platonic male friend is the man you go out with just to have fun. You do not take advantage of his kindness and you always make an effort to pay your own way, or even treat him every now and then. It is dating without all the drama! You can enjoy outings without worrying about how you look or if he thinks your outfit is cute. The only downside is that when either one of you enters into a serious relationship with someone else, that person may not be overjoyed by the close friendship you share, and could well try to put an end to all your fun together. You must also make sure that this man knows that he is just a friend, or you might inadvertently be stringing him along. Perhaps the best way to guard against this is to choose a gay man as your platonic male friend – that way everyone knows exactly where they stand.

## One-night Stand

In a way, a one-night stand is the ultimate form of sexual liberation for women. Whilst men may have been having casual sex for centuries, for women it is still a relatively new experience, and as

I said before what you do with your own body is entirely your own business. Having said that, there does appear to be a growing trend among young women for having casual sex. This could well be an extreme rebellion against centuries of sexual restraint. However, when this type of behaviour becomes a lifestyle, I feel that it is ultimately damaging to a woman's self-esteem and it can put her health and personal safety at risk.

A one-night stand does not make someone a bad person. Anyone can get carried away and may find themselves in a situation they had not planned. Mistakes are how we learn, but waking up next to a total stranger, with no memory of how you got there, means that you were in a very vulnerable position. This type of casual sex could be regarded as the 'fast-food' aspect of sexual encounters – it is quick, it is easy, it is readily available and if you are lucky it might even be satisfying. But it is certainly not healthy. Many unplanned pregnancies occur due to a combination of alcohol intake and casual sex. Add to this the fact the sexually transmitted diseases such as chlamydia and gonorrhoea are on the increase, and it is fairly safe to say that casual sex as a lifestyle choice is a toxic situation. Factor in the rape drug Rohypnol or Roofies and date rape also becomes a very real danger, particularly if you are in the habit of accepting drinks from strangers or going home with people you hardly know.

If you find that casual sex has become more of a routine event rather than the odd occurrence, then you need to do some soul searching to discover why you are behaving in this manner. Going out 'on the pull' might feel a bit daring to begin with, but if this type of thrill seeking becomes a habit you are actually putting yourself at risk. Learn to value yourself more. Respect yourself and your body. Even if you claim to enjoy such a lifestyle there are likely to be times when you feel used and unfulfilled by such encounters.

One-night stands might be a fact of modern society but they certainly do not help women connect with the inner goddess. As a goddess incarnate try to be discriminating in your choice of partners. Just because a man asks you out and you have a great time and enjoy his company does not mean that you need to sleep with him right away. Take your time, and value the sexual experience as the sacred act it is.

## Phone Sex

Phone sex can be a very enjoyable experience, and it is a fantastic way of connecting with your lover over a long distance. If your partner is working away, or you live apart, there will undoubtedly be occasions when you are feeling frisky and you miss him like crazy. Phone sex is the answer. It involves fantasy story telling, dirty sex talk and masturbation. It can be fun and saucy and will give you a nice private joke to smile about when you do get back together again.

It goes without saying that it should be a mutual experience, so you should not allow yourself to be distracted by the latest soap opera! Hints that a phone sex session may be on the cards are questions such as 'Are you in bed? What are you wearing?' Feel free to tell a few sexy fibs here; if you are in your old pyjamas and novelty slippers tell him you are in a black leather catsuit and boots! Phone sex is all about fantasy so make sure you give him something he can work with. Although the telephone creates a barrier between you this can actually be very liberating as you are less likely to be embarrassed when exploring your fantasies.

You should really only be having phone sex with your partner; phone sex infidelity may not qualify as actual cheating but it is a very low trick. And such conversations should be entirely private so do not record them. It is also the height of bad manners to answer call waiting, pick up your mobile or send a text message to someone while indulging in phone sex.

Sexy text messaging is also a kind of phone sex, and it can help to set the tone and build up the drama for the real session or an actual date. Phone sex can help to enhance the depth of intimacy you share with your lover and it is the best kind of goodnight call.

## Girl about Town

The freedom of life as a single, child-free woman means that you are not tied to the house in any way. Your wings are unclipped and you can fly where you will. A single woman has no one else to consider and her day is her own to fill as she wishes. Obviously a single mother has less freedom as she has her child's needs to consider, but she can still enjoy going out with her friends or with a man.

As a single woman you are free to live your life to the full. Factor in some exciting events for your rest and relaxation days and you will begin to see your life as a varied and colourful rainbow of delights. Here are a few tips to help you stay safe when you are out and about.

- Always use your own car, or get a lift with a trusted friend. Keep your car doors locked at all times. If you must use public transport sit as close to the driver as possible, or use a reputable taxi company.
- Keep your mobile phone with you and fully charged at all times.
- Always keep hold of your drink; never accept drinks from strangers or leave your drink unattended. Do not drink so much alcohol that you become vulnerable and at risk.
- Have your door key ready for a swift entrance to your home, ensuring that no one is behind you or loitering nearby before you actually open the door. When you are home alone keep the doors locked and do not answer the door unless you are sure you know who it is.
- Do not give out your phone number, address or personal details. Maintain your privacy and shred all papers to guard against identity theft and vital information getting into the wrong hands.
- Do not go home with or leave a venue with strangers or someone you do not know well.

- Always practise safe sex.
- Use your intuition; if someone or something makes you feel uncomfortable then leave immediately.
- Plan your event or evening in detail and try not to leave anything to chance. Know how you will get there, where you will meet friends and how you will get home again.
- Always carry enough money to cover a taxi fare home in case of emergency or the need to make a speedy exit.
- Look out for your friends. At least one of you should remain sober.

## Going It Alone

Nothing is more empowering than going out totally alone – no boyfriend, no girlfriends, no meeting up with someone at the venue, just you alone, doing something you enjoy. It is the ultimate declaration of independence and, if all your friends are entrenched in marital and motherhood bliss, it can often be the best option. Why should you wait on anyone else's life? I am not saying that you should never go out with married friends, but be realistic; it might be difficult for them to enjoy the kind of social freedom you take for granted. Their priorities have changed. This means that your priorities must change too, and rather than going out as a group, you may end up going alone. Why make your friends feel guilty because they cannot go with you, when you can simply book a ticket for one and enjoy yourself?

I often go out to events on my own. It is one of the best aspects of a free and independent lifestyle and when I am sitting absorbed in the ballet or watching a film at the cinema I enjoy it just as much as when I go with friends. And there is something incredibly romantic about dating yourself – at least you know that you will show up and you will not cancel at the last minute! You also never know who you might meet; a woman alone at the theatre has an enigmatic presence. Going out alone will make you feel very independent and autonomous and it will make you realize that you do not need anyone else in order to enjoy your life. Every so often make the effort to go out entirely on your own. The more you do this the more you will come to realize just how free you are, and you will appreciate your liberty that much more.

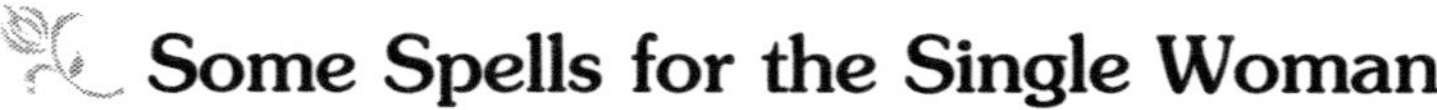

## Some Spells for the Single Woman

### *Protection*

For this spell you will need a small tiger's eye crystal and some sea salt. On the night of the full moon place the crystal in the centre of a large plate and surround it with an unbroken circle of sea salt. Hold your hands over the crystal, palms down and chant:

*Goddess Bast of feline grace*
*Enchant this crystal through time and space.*
*Protect and guard me every day,*
*Keep me safe from being prey.*
*Independently I live my life.*
*Guard me from all forms of strife,*
*Autonomous, wise and totally free*
*Enjoying my sweet liberty!*

Leave the salt and crystal in place for a complete lunar cycle, then put the crystal in your purse and carry it with you at all times.

### *To Summon a Lover*

Light a tea-light and place it in a suitable holder. Then write this incantation on a slip of paper using a red pen.

*As a flower attracts the honey bee*
*I summon a lover to come to me.*
*Beneath the light of the lover's moon*
*Sweet Goddess grant to me this boon.*

*In the name of maiden, mother, crone*
*By my will it shall be done!*

Say it three times and then light the spell paper in the tea-light and let it burn in a heat proof bowl. Allow the tea-light to burn down naturally on your love goddess altar. A lover should come to you within three moons.

## To Turn a Fling into a Relationship

This spell will only work if both parties want the liaison to progress. Cut out two paper hearts and write your own name on one and your lover's name on the other. Light a red candle and drip some of the wax on to the heart with your lover's name and say:

*The heat of passion will enflame*
*A deeper love, in witchcraft's name!*

Place the heart bearing your own name on top of the molten wax, sticking the two hearts together. Then say:

*Your heart for me, my heart for you*
*Together in love, stuck like glue.*
*For the free will of all, this spell will be*
*Or else I set this lover free.*

Leave the spell hearts on your love altar and allow the candle to burn down naturally. For the best results perform the spell on the night of the full moon, preferably in the spring when nature is renewed with life and love.

***Add a teaspoon of golden honey to a hot bath to smooth your skin and increase your powers of natural feminine attraction.***

## Siren Secret

*An independent spirit is a very sexy asset to have and single girls can make the very most of their freedom while still engaging in a romantic liaison or two. This type of single life is a far cry from the 'old maid' existence of centuries past; these days a single girl can enjoy the very best of both worlds. So if co-habiting and conventional commitment are not for you, then make a declaration of personal independence. Autonomy is alluring and very sexy indeed so take a few positive steps forward and start living the life of a single temptress!*

CHAPTER 12

# An Affair to Remember

Before you make the assumption that this is a 'have your cake and eat it' chapter, let me just say that I do not condone cheating or extramarital affairs. If a relationship is no longer working for you then you should have the courage to tell your partner that it is over before you begin to see someone else. That said I am fully aware that affairs do happen and that people will come up with any number of reasons to excuse their dishonest conduct. But if your relationship is so bad that you are considering cheating, then why are you still in the relationship in the first place? Most women are now financially independent from their husbands or at least have the opportunity to be so by pursuing their own careers. And divorce is hard on children of any age, so waiting until they are old enough to understand will not make the collapse of their family any easier for them to deal with. If the relationship is bad, end it.

The simple fact is that there is no decent excuse for cheating. While you might convince yourself that you have no other option and that no one will be hurt, the truth is that unless you are a spectacular liar, the affair will be discovered at some stage and it is likely to leave a trail of devastation in its wake. Old wounds may not heal, so even if you give the relationship another try, there will be an underlying current of resentment and once the trust is gone it can be very difficult, if not impossible, to win it back. And if you know how easy it is to cheat you might never trust anyone again, and might judge the behaviour of others by your own indiscretion!

So how do you save your relationship from the talons of a home wrecker? And how do you find the thrills in your relationship before you become tempted to seek them elsewhere? First, though, which side of the love triangle you are on: are you the one having the affair, or the one being cheated on? Each scenario requires a different kind of response, of course.

## The Wronged Woman

Anyone can be betrayed; whether or not you happen to be married is irrelevant. It will not lessen the pain or sense of loss if you are just dating or living together. If you discover or suspect that your partner is being unfaithful then you need to put some boundaries in place in order to protect yourself as much as possible. By this I mean that you need a battle plan. Are you going to confront him outright or would you prefer to bide your time and gather evidence of his infidelity? Can you bear to continue living with a man who has lied to you, and could you come to trust him again? Or do you prefer to end the relationship and strike out on your own? If you do, will you leave the shared home or will he?

These are all very difficult questions to ask yourself, but the clearer you are at this stage the stronger your position will be. It is essential that you do what is best for you, and not what your partner might be asking you to do – he lost all right to ask you anything when he cheated. In having a battle plan at the ready you will be better prepared for the showdown which is likely to come and you will be able to get through the ordeal with dignity. You can fall apart later, in private, but for now do not give him the satisfaction of seeing how devastated you are – he is not worthy of your tears. Making the break is always the hardest part, and picking yourself up afterwards will take time, but it will be worth it in the end when you are making a success of your life without him; remember the old adage, 'living well is the best revenge!'

## The Paramour

If you are seeing a man you know to be married or involved then you need to accept that you will always be in second place; even if at a later stage he ends his relationship to be with you, he will have developed a pattern of putting you off for the sake of other commitments, and this is likely to continue. It may be that he treats you like a queen when you are together, that he is charming and affectionate. But why would you want to settle for being second best? You would never eat a stranger's leftover food, so why accept another woman's sexual leftovers into your bed? Surely you are worth more?

It could be that he spoils you with gifts and flowers, expensive dinners and so on. Or perhaps you only see him when he is feeling frisky – he might treat your home as a risk-free brothel and after a 'quickie' he is away back to his wife. The sex could be fantastic, but can you be sure that he is not treating his wife to the encore performance? Some people claim that an affair actually improves the sex within the original relationship as the cheater is eager to try out new bedroom tricks on their long term partner.

Being in second place will mean that his home life will always come first. He might let you down and cancel events at the last minute, or it might feel as if you are constantly trying to scratch a few moments from his busy life. The time you do spend together might be very rushed, leaving you frustrated and cross. Would you not prefer to be with a single man who makes you his main priority, giving you his full and undivided attention? Would you not prefer a man who is not constantly going home to his partner and putting you on the back burner in favour of his family?

If a quick fling is all you want then take into consideration the possibility that his wife may discover her partner's infidelity, and kick him out of the marital home; he might land then on your doorstep, bags and all. This could turn out to be more than you bargained for and you could finish up in a relationship when all you wanted was a bit of fun. Masculine nature being what it is he might waste no time in taking over your home and calling all the shots. Your life could become his territory, and when you protest he might complain that he gave up everything to be with you!

Of course he could leave his partner by choice to be with you, and this might be a great boost to your ego; you might even be flattered and regard it as a compliment. Think it through a little further, however: how do you know you can really trust him? If he cheated on his wife with you, will he eventually cheat on you too? Is there any truth in the saying, 'Once a cheater always a cheater'? Are you prepared to take the risk? And could you face the possible showdown with his wife?

Being someone's mistress might seem like a romantic option and a stab at independence and sexual liberty, but it is not conducive to improving your self-esteem, nor is it likely to ensure that your lover treats you with the respect you deserve. If you are content to be the runner up and share your man with another woman, then you need to do some serious soul searching to find out why; do you not think that you deserve more?

## Tempted to Cheat

It can be all too easy to assume that it is usually men who cheat, but woman can be just as unfaithful. In any long-term relationship the day-to-day monotony can make your life together seem stale and your sex life predictable. It might be that you can anticipate all the moves your partner makes, but that does not mean than an affair is going to offer you the fulfilment you are secretly craving. While it is quite natural to find someone other than your partner attractive and enjoy a little innocent flirtation, if you find yourself hoping to be alone with someone or looking for ways to bump into them then you have officially entered the danger zone!

While it can be flattering that someone other than your partner is making a play for your attentions, if you are truly tempted by such an offer and willing to put your relationship at risk then you need to find out why. What is wrong with your current relationship that you should consider seeking solace elsewhere? Perhaps it is simply the excitement that you find enticing? But if deep down you want to get out of your relationship then there are much kinder and more dignified ways of doing so.

If you are still in love with your partner but bored by your sex life then the answer could be even simpler; your partner is probably feeling just as bored with the situation so talk it over and discover new ways to put the fizz back into your sex. Rediscover the fulfilment which you used to feel together. Try out the hints, tips and spells in this book or visit an erotic emporium to kick-start your imagination.

## Mistresses of the Past

Extramarital affairs are by no means confined to modern society. In the past cheating was common and in a world where divorce was frowned upon, the wronged spouse had little choice but to turn a blind eye to such infidelities.

While the courtesans were at the very top of their tree and could mingle with high society and royalty, the lorette played a more precarious game; her security was far from assured. A lorette was the lover of a powerful man in a position of wealth. She was the mistress or kept woman of her day. Rather than selling her favours to many clients like the courtesans, she was the lover of one man in particular and there was often a romantic attachment.

While the life of a lorette was not as lavish as that of a courtesan, she by no means lived in poverty; her lover would usually provide her with a nice home, fashionable clothing etc. However, while the courtesans were admired from afar the situation of a lorette was less enviable. She existed on the very edge of society, walking a very fine line between acceptance and social ostracism. She was usually far more dependent on her lover than a courtesan would have been; she was the original 'other woman', and her role has often been romanticized in literature – for example Tolstoy's tragic heroine Anna Karenina.

These days the lorette can be likened to the mistresses of high-profile celebrities, 'kiss and tell' girls and those who make a career off the back of their sexploits. To a large extent all the romanticism has been lost, and the life of a mistress is not nearly as glamorous as it once was.

## Keeping Your Lover Faithful

How do you prevent your relationship from going stale and becoming vulnerable to an affair? The simple answer is to do all you can to keep your sex life and overall relationship as interesting as possible, so that neither one of you will feel the need to seek sexual solace elsewhere.

Obviously there will always be the odd love rat (and not just men) who makes a regular habit of cheating. But in most healthy relationships an affair is usually the result of some form of neglect. If someone feels unloved, unappreciated, ignored or taken for granted, if their needs are not being met by their current partner, then it is only a matter of time before a third party offers to fill the void. Here are some ideas to keep your relationship interesting and exciting.

### *'I am every Woman'*

Keep your partner interested by becoming a master of disguise. Use your imagination to take on a persona or to explore certain facets of your character. If you wear jeans and a T-shirt every day and your idea of dressing up is putting on your 'good jeans', not only will you look boring and unimaginative but your partner may begin to regard you as being totally predictable.

As most men are turned on visually give him something interesting to look at. Take your inspiration from stars such as Madonna and Kylie Minogue, who are both famous for reinventing themselves and changing their image to present a different persona. There is absolutely no reason why you cannot do this too. Become a chameleon in your attitude to clothes and keep him fascinated by becoming a different woman each day; go from 'girl next door' to rock chick; from chic romantic to 'up for it tomboy'; from fragile shy violet to vampy vixen; from glamorous Hitchcock heroine to sexy Wiccan siren. Dress in as many different looks as you can imagine and fascinate him by being every type of girl he has ever dreamed of in one. By ensuring that he is never quite sure which you he will be waking up next to you are sparking his interest on a daily basis and so renewing the flame of passion.

### *'Do you come here often?'*

If all else fails have an affair – with each other! This can be great fun and it will certainly take the monotony out of your relationship. Arrange to meet in a hotel bar, having first booked a room. Arrive separately and then act as though you have never met before. This is your very first meeting, so you should introduce yourselves accordingly. But here is the fun part: invent a completely new character and play out that role. So rather than being Mrs Wright, mother of three and loyal housewife, become Selena Carter, air hostess, or someone equally glamorous and exciting. Your partner could go from being a computer programmer to a fighter pilot or a fireman, or whatever his secret ambition is. You could even dress accordingly, hiring costumes from a fancy dress store. Have a good chat and get to know one another in character and then retire to your room for a 'one-night stand'. Leave the hotel separately and return to your normal lives. This kind of activity will give you both the thrill of an affair without either one of you having to actually cheat.

Once you have established your fantasy characters play the name game by sending each other sexy texts, emails, etc. under the name of your alias. This will keep the fantasy alive and fizzing until you can arrange another meeting. Also try sending chocolates and flowers and arranging the odd dirty weekend.

# Fidelity Spells

For centuries certain rituals have been performed to ensure fidelity from a partner. From the exchanging of rings, which are a symbol of eternity and a visual indication that you are off the market, to the romantic tradition of exchanging locks of hair, fidelity magic has as much relevance today as it had in the past. Try out the following spells to give your relationship the best chance of faithful longevity.

*Fruit of Love.* Magical tradition states that sharing an apple with your lover will ensure that you remain faithful to one another. Choose a shiny red apple if at all possible, and cut it in half across the equator line; this will reveal the seeds and you will notice that they form the shape of a five-pointed star or pentagram. Now give one half of the apple to your lover and eat the other half yourself to complete the fidelity magic.

*Lover's Locks Entwined.* Cut a small lock of your lover's hair, and a similar lock of your own, then bind them together using red cotton. Place the bound locks in a special place, for example in the box which contained your engagement or wedding ring, or with your marriage certificate. Do not lose or unbind the hair unless the relationship has come to a natural end, and keep it safe for the duration of the relationship.

*Holly and Ivy.* This fidelity spell also has fertility powers so it is ideal if you want to start a family. Cut a stem of holly and a length of ivy and twine the ivy around the holly to ensure fidelity and fertility in your relationship. Place them beneath the bed and leave them there.

*To Prevent a Partner from Straying.* This traditional ritual is said to keep a partner from straying to a rival's home and being unfaithful. Smear a small amount of honey on to the soles of your lover's shoes and let them sit in the light of the full moon overnight. Just do not use so much honey that he sticks to the pavement the following day!

## Temptress Tip

*It can be easy in a long-term relationship to forget to make time for one another. This is especially the case when you have a career, a home and a family to look after as you will be scratching for time. But it is vital to the success of your relationship that you make the effort to look nice and spend quality time with your partner. Be the sexy miss that he fell in love with, not the frumpy, grumpy mother who is too tired to appreciate her man. Be sexy and seductive and make him realize just how gorgeous you are and how much you love and appreciate him.*

## Siren Secret

*It is quite wrong to believe that having an affair will hurt no one, or that it need not affect your core relationship and family life. It is probably the very worst damage you can inflict on any relationship and few relationships can weather such a storm.*

*A Wiccan temptress does not prey on married or attached men. She has no desire to share a lover's time with another woman and would much rather enjoy the undivided attentions of a single man. Her high level of self-respect means that if an affair does happen to touch her life in some way, she weathers the storm with dignity and poise, and then moves swiftly on.*

CHAPTER 13

# Living the Life of a Temptress

When a woman decides to take the way of the Wiccan temptress she is in effect reclaiming her sacred femininity and her goddess-given magic. Living a goddess-centred life means that you are honouring your allure and your sexuality on a daily basis without any of the shame, embarrassment or guilt which centuries of patriarchy has attempted to instil in womankind.

Being sexy and seductive is not simply a matter of having sex and making yourself available to masculine attentions. As I have said, a woman can be completely celibate or a virgin and still be regarded as a temptress. Her seductiveness is not in her availability; rather it comes from a personal attitude which promotes feelings of confidence, empowerment and a sense of divine inner beauty.

By embracing her inner temptress in a sacred, magical way a woman tends to become much stronger in herself and more in control of her own destiny, for she is tapping into her natural power. By acknowledging her sexuality as a great gift she is less likely to indulge in inappropriate behaviour, or to accept derogatory treatment, abuse or sexual pressure from men. Nor is she likely to remain in a destructive relationship or settle for second best because she is afraid to be alone. Rather she will embrace her independence, rediscover her adventurous spirit and take on all that the world has to offer with her goddess-given charms.

Such an attitude can actually bring a woman much closer to the divine feminine, making it easier to connect with the Goddess during ritual work and spell craft. This divine interaction can serve to reinforce the feminine power, increasing self-assurance and self-worth on a regular basis. Working spells of seduction magic can envelop a woman in an aura of mystery and magnetism. The effort the Wiccan temptress makes with her personal appearance will ensure that she is never overlooked or invisible, but is always offered opportunities and help when she needs them. Her inner poise, self-reliance and polished appearance mean that she is more likely to be considered for promotion at work. Simply put, a sexy woman gets ahead – not because she is writhing around on life's casting couch, but because her attunement with her natural allure gives her a sense of fortitude, while her independent spirit makes her self-reliant and responsible. These are all qualities employers are on the look-out for.

It is always worth remembering that seduction magic can enhance a woman's overall power; it is not confined to her role in the bedroom. The essence of magnetism which seduction magic gives to a woman can be carried over and used to great advantage in other areas of her life too.

## Sweet Seductresses of Mythology

Mythology and goddess tradition are rich with examples of the powerful temptress at work. From the mythologies of Greece, Rome and the Celts to Arthurian sagas, the temptress has her place in all of them. Here is a brief introduction to some of the greatest seductresses ever to have found their way on to the printed page. I have also included their traditional powers and attributes in magic so that you can invoke them into your personal rituals if you wish.

## Aphrodite

Mighty Aphrodite was the powerful Greek goddess of love, passion and beauty. She was born of the sea, carried on waves and swept into shore by Zephyrus, the west wind. She landed on the isle of Cyprus, where her name is still well known today and statues of her are sold by the thousands to tourists. Her association with the sea, sun and sand make her the patron goddess of the holiday romance. She tends to indulge in the more frivolous side of love, urging us to have fun with one another, to enjoy the act of love for its own sake and think about the consequences tomorrow. This is the goddess who made Paris and Helen of Troy fall in love, bringing them together in a union which would begin the Trojan War.

Aphrodite's ocean birth means that she is associated with mermaids and sirens, who were her handmaidens. She can be represented on an altar with sea shells, or beeswax candles, as the honey bee is sacred to her. Anything made with honey can be left as an offering to her. A pot of golden honey placed near the bed can help to make sex much sweeter! Indeed, as mentioned earlier, some men still refer to a woman's vagina as the golden honey pot, proving that echoes from this goddess have passed down through the centuries. Call on Aphrodite to enhance your beauty, improve your love life or bring about a fun holiday romance.

## Venus

Venus is the Roman counterpart to Aphrodite a goddess of love and beauty, but she encourages the serious side of love – companionship, togetherness, mutual support. Her role includes all love, not just the romantic variety. She is associated with spring flowers and the summer rose and her festival falls on 1 April. To commune with Venus place roses on your altar and burn a rose-fragranced oil or incense. Call on her to deepen a relationship or to help you to communicate more effectively with family and friends.

## Diana

Diana is the Roman huntress goddess of the moon. She is a chaste virgin goddess and is a guardian of female chastity and celibacy. She protects woman and children from any kind of masculine abuse, and she is also the patron goddess of childbirth. Diana was the original feminist! She is associated with woodlands and forest where the hunt took place and her sacred creatures include deer, hounds and stags, the hunter and the hunted.

Tradition states that Diana liked to bathe in a natural pool in a forest glade beneath the light of the full moon, and lochs and lakes are still referred to as Diana's mirrors. She is generally depicted carrying a bow and arrows, and she is sometimes shown with that other great hunter, the cat, another of her sacred animals. This feline association meant that Diana became known as the goddess of witches.

One myth tells how Diana was bathing naked in her favourite pool when a young huntsman came upon the pool and watched her; she was so furious she turned him into a stag and he was ripped apart by his own hounds. She is not a goddess to mess with!

Call on Diana at the time of the full moon to help you define and maintain your independence, to guard your privacy and even to protect yourself from nosy neighbours. She can also assist you through any period of celibacy you decide to take and she can give you the strength to break free from a bad relationship.

## Persephone

Persephone is the Greek goddess of springtime; her mother, Demeter, is the goddess of summer. Together they rule over the lighter half of the year. One day Hades, the god of the underworld, saw Persephone and fell in love with her, so he stole her away to his underworld kingdom. Demeter fell into a deep depression at the loss of her daughter and autumn and winter swept over the land.

Meanwhile in the underworld Persephone was being wooed. Knowing her responsibility as goddess of spring she did not wish to stay in the underworld for ever, yet the opportunity to be Hades' queen and gain some independence from her mother was too good to pass up! In compromise Persephone ate six seeds of the pomegranate Hades gave her; this meant that she spent six months of the year with Hades as queen of the underworld, and six months in the world above with her mother, creating spring and summer together. Thus the seasons are broken into the lighter half of spring and summer and the darker half of autumn and winter.

You can attune with Persephone by leaving a pomegranate on your altar or by drinking pomegranate juice. Call on her for assistance with issues of independence from parental interference and when dealing with unwanted attention from unsuitable admirers.

Please note the above is my interpretation of the Persephone myth.

## *Circe*

Circe is the dark enchantress of Greek mythology. She lived on the island of Aeaea where Odysseus and his men were swept ashore in a violent storm on their voyage home from the Trojan War. She made the men most welcome, offering them goblets of enchanted wine which turned them into swine. Only Odysseus was immune, so Circe seduced him with other charms instead, taking him to her bed and persuading him to remain on the island for a while. He accepted on condition that Circe removed the enchantment from his men. She did so, and allowed them to feast themselves back to good health before they all left to complete the journey home.

Although not the nicest of goddesses Circe does have her uses in magic. She can be called upon to help you through a bad break-up, banish an ex-lover who will not go away or bring justifiable retribution to an unfaithful lover. Just remember to cast all spells with harm to none, especially when invoking this tricky enchantress.

## *Isis*

Isis is the Egyptian goddess of birth, death, rebirth, fertility and motherhood. She is a skilled sorceress and practitioner of magic.

She was the wife of Osiris and when he was killed by Seth she recovered his body, embalmed it and then brought him back to life using magic. Her sacred animals are the serpent and the cow. Her powers can be invoked if you want to move your relationship towards marriage and motherhood. She can offer protection during pregnancy and childbirth and she can strengthen you as you face the trials of motherhood.

## Rhiannon

Rhiannon is a horse goddess of Celtic mythology. Pwyll the prince of Dyfed was sitting on magical hill known as the Mound of Arberth, hoping that he would experience a vision when Rhiannon rode past him on her beautiful white faerie steed. Pwyll quickly tried to follow her but no matter how fast he went he could not catch up. Then he realized that she was from the magical realm of Annwn. Eventually he called out for her to stop and she did so. The two fell madly in love and eventually married but they were destined to be unhappy, for following the death of their first child Rhiannon was accused of infanticide and was cursed to tell her mournful tale to all who would listen. Pwyll's love remained true, but Rhiannon was ultimately being punished for marrying a mortal man.

This is Rhiannon's romantic side, but she has a darker aspect too for she is also the white night mare who brings terrifying visions in sleep. In this aspect she is said to bless writers and poets with inspiration, only to line her bed with their bones upon their death.

As a goddess of seduction you can call on Rhiannon to help bring about love at first sight – although there are no guarantees of a happy ending! She can also help if you are writing love letters or poetry for your beloved.

## Guinevere

Guinevere is the wife of King Arthur in the Arthurian legends. As is well known, she fell madly in love with her champion, Sir Lancelot, a knight of the round table. As a goddess icon Guinevere could be said to be demonstrating her sexual freedom in taking Lancelot to be her lover, but although there are variations of the legend the outcome is not usually a happy one. Perhaps this is because the early legends were usually written by men, who wanted to punish the unfaithful wife! Invoking Guinevere as a magical archetype can help you if you need to make a choice between two suitors. Attuning with her energies can help you to come to the right decision in making your final choice of mate. Her sacred creature is the white owl so try meditating on a picture of a snowy owl to connect with this archetype.

## *Isolde*

Isolde is another heroine goddess of Celtic mythology. As the princess of Ireland, she was not in a position to marry for love. When Sir Tristan came to Ireland from Cornwall to beg her hand on behalf of his uncle King Mark, she had little say in the matter. Her nurse gave her a flask of wine to share with her new husband on their wedding night, but Isolde, who had fallen in love with Tristan, shared it with him instead. It contained a strong love potion and the two lovers betrayed King Mark by their illicit affair.

Again there are variations of the tale, but as a goddess archetype Isolde can help magical practitioners who are in love with the wrong man, or who are suffering from the pangs of unrequited love. Isolde's symbol is the Irish shamrock so meditate on this image when you seek her guidance and support.

## *Morgan le Fey*

Morgan le Fey is the dark enchantress of the Authurian legends. Just as King Arthur is sometimes associated with the summer, so Morgan is the winter goddess. She has close links with the Lady of the Lake, and as her name suggests, with the water sirens known as 'Morgans'. In some schools of thought Morgan le Fey is said to derive from the Celtic battle goddess the Morrigan, and there are certainly similarities between the two characters.